Full Bloom, Victoria Bedford Betts.

EXPLORING FINGER PAINT

BY VICTORIA BEDFORD BETTS

Davis Publications, Inc.
WORCESTER, MASSACHUSETTS

5266

FOREWORD . . .

Since the early thirties, when Victoria Bedford Betts first met and assisted Ruth Faison Shaw, the originator of finger painting, she has been exploring and teaching with finger paint.

No one today is better qualified to write about this medium and its many forms and uses than the author. She has studied and worked with students of all ages to observe their manipulations and creations with finger paint and with other art media. In addition, she has taught thousands of teachers in her former position as Art Consultant for Binney & Smith Inc., and as Director of their New York Studio. Her paintings have been exhibited in two solo exhibits and in countless group shows; her designs applied to greeting cards and displays, and her free-flowing demonstrations used in films and on television.

In EXPLORING FINGER PAINT, the author has maintained a creative approach while offering many well defined suggestions and processes. The book provides answers for questions raised by the novice as well as stimulations for the experienced painter.

The author's enthusiasm for finger paint cannot help but catch and hold the interest of the reader and inspire him to experiment, create and invent new ways of working with finger paint and other materials. As Victoria Bedford Betts states with conviction and authority, "No medium should be approached with limited vision."

This work is well organized, informative and is augmented with over two hundred illustrations. It is an invaluable resource book for those who desire to explore, discover and invent with finger paint.

ROSEMARY BEYMER, *Director*,
Department of Art Education,
Kansas City, Missouri.

INTRODUCTION . . .

This book, like the book EXPLORING PAPIER-MÂCHÉ by the same author, is one that encourages experiments with materials. In this book, Victoria Bedford Betts describes the process as initially presented and shows the development of finger painting growing out of a need for a medium with its unique qualities.

Motivation needs are realized and many suggestions are offered. Problems of organization and care of materials, evaluation and exhibition are presented to stimulate thinking rather than to solve all possible problems.

Finger painting explorations show that here is a medium suitable to all age levels. Teachers should be aware of its scope as well as its limitations. As in experiences with other materials, a suspicious or timid approach may hinder enjoyment and learning. The author hopes that all teachers will recognize the need for a happy approach to art experiences and the need for a variety of experiences.

EXPLORING FINGER PAINT has several aims. One is to record the history of the medium and experiences by students, teachers and artists in the past twenty-eight years. Another is to encourage inventions and sincere expressions by the guidance and understanding of well-trained teachers. The last is to relive the wonderful memories of many years of finger painting with all ages and all kinds of people.

ACKNOWLEDGMENTS . . .

Many friends and colleagues have cooperated, wholeheartedly, in the preparation of EXPLORING FINGER PAINT by offering their time and experience. To all of them I wish to express my sincere gratitude and appreciation for their ideas and also for their gracious loans of artists' and students' work for use as illustrations.

In addition, I am especially indebted to the following contributors who encouraged the progress of the manuscript with competent and concrete assistance:

Ruth Faison Shaw, for guidance and inspiration as well as for the loan of historical information and illustrative material;

Binney and Smith Inc., and its staff of Art Consultants and Studio Assistants, for their many explorations and accompanying photographic records;

William H. Milliken, Jr., for initiating the writing of this book and his encouragement to complete it;

School Arts Magazine and its contributors, for helpful illustrations of children's and teachers' work;

Charles L. Betts, my husband, for patiently photographing hundreds of explorations;

Henry Ray, for his enthusiasm and for photographing countless paintings;

Henry Ahrens, for explorations, for reading the complete manuscript and for assistance in the selection of illustrations;

Ann Franco Ferreira Thompson, for her effective and efficient pen-and-ink work in Chapter Eleven, for her creative teaching, and for the loan of experiments by her students;

Catherine M. Pilley, for her zeal and patience in typing many drafts of the text;

My students, of all ages, who have contributed to my education and to this text.

V. B. B.

Landscape, Genevieve Cody.

CONTENTS . . .

Ruth Faison Shaw, Chapel Hill, North Carolina.

Chapter One
HISTORY OF FINGER PAINTING

Finger painting is one of the oldest forms of art. Paradoxically, it is also one of the newest. Prehistoric caves in France and Etruscan tombs bear evidence of its uses. Painted surfaces of Pompeii still show the texture of hands.

The Chinese painter, Chung Isao, is regarded by some as the inventor of the finger-painting process in the year 750. Later, several Chinese artists who applied the method were Kao Chi Pei (1672–1732), Teng Kui, a century later, and, in 1939, Professor Y. K. Chang of Soochow University. With the Chinese, the thumb and finger tips were used as brushes and the paintings had the characteristics of Oriental brush work with water color as the medium.

It was not until 1929, when a special paint was invented for the method, that finger painting in its present day technique came into being. That year, in her school for English-speaking children in Rome, Italy, an American teacher, Ruth Faison Shaw, compounded a paint formula harmless to stomach and skin. Her patience and perseverance gave us a paint which, when used as initially presented, recorded movements and impressions of fingers, hands and arms.

Two Egrets.
A finger painting by Y. K. Chang.

3

Madonna and Child, Peggy, Age 12, Rome, 1932.

Four Saints of the Church, Edith, Age 12, Rome, 1932.

At the Shaw School in Rome, the finger-painting technique was developed as a joint adventure of teacher and students. It all began with a child's cut finger. With the wet iodine which had been applied, he painted on a door. Miss Shaw's receptive mind was kindled by the memory of his enjoyment and fanned to produce a suitable medium. Finger-painting activities soon received world-wide attention; Miss Shaw was invited to discuss her work at educational conferences in France, England and America.

Settled in New York City a few years later, Ruth Shaw taught at the Dalton School and opened the Shaw Finger-paint Studio to devote her time to spreading the "gospel" of creative teaching. Fragments of a talk given by her in 1933 show an understanding and knowledge of child education:

> *"In the elementary school, all things should be taught on which future study will be based. The elementary teacher should prepare the ground for the specialist teacher. She should teach principles, not details. In addition, she should continually persevere in educating herself and get much of this education from the very children she teaches."*
>
> *"All this has an important bearing on finger painting. For its purpose is rather to prepare the ground for future specialized work than act as a specialized course in itself. What is the purpose of teaching? For me it is to equip the child with three qualities necessary for his or her future character; the ability to create from within; from without to receive, and through the bridge of adaptability, to unite the first two."*

The early thirties were pioneering years for Miss Shaw and her helpers, among them: Stuart Shaw, Ralph Reasor, Cyril Brown, Sara Ravndal and Victoria Bedford. Finger paint was made by

The Studio Staff in 1951.
Photograph by Phyllis Twachtman.
New York World-Telegram and Sun.

various helpers in a small factory on New York City's East River and moved in a wheelbarrow, by moonlight, to the Shaw Studio, a few blocks away, where labels were attached, sheets of paper counted, and finger-paint sets assembled for distribution to schools. The demand for finger paint grew; children loved it, and it became increasingly popular as an adult medium for recreation and art expression.

Many changes were begun in 1936: Binney and Smith started to manufacture the paint, and the Shaw Studio moved to their offices, then on 42nd Street and Madison Avenue in New York City; teachers were welcomed at the Studio for lessons in finger painting; exhibits of children's work and of professional artists were loaned to schools; Ruth Shaw and a staff of art consultants traveled the country to explain the medium and the method.

The recognition of the value of the medium encouraged many manufacturers to make similar products, but the vision of Ruth Faison Shaw and her associates, including the officers and representatives of Binney and Smith Inc., should be recorded in finger-painting history as the first and most zealous exponents of this art medium in America.

Twins, Chris and Carol Ravndal, Age 3,
Little Silver, New Jersey, 1939.

5

Photograph, Courtesy of Eugenia C. Nowlin, Chief, Army Crafts Unit, Recreation Section, Washington, D. C.

Atlantic Convoy, Stanley Mazurk.

Photograph, courtesy of William H. Milliken, Jr.

During World War II the workshop plan of participation proved far more helpful than expert demonstrations alone. Teachers welcomed in-service training, and, in turn, many relayed their training to Red Cross and USO workers and volunteers. Servicemen became students in hospitals and service clubs and, through their enjoyment in finger painting, many continued to create with other painting and craft materials.

Post-war years saw an increasing demand for art education workshops in materials. Aims and objectives were to break down inhibitions, encourage good work habits, show the varied quality of art activity, emphasize the original use of materials and initiate or encourage the workshop plan for continuous learning.

Workshop participation by thousands of teachers developed an awareness of the almost unlimited uses of finger paint and other art materials.

Increased knowledge of materials led to mixed media explorations and to activities using the finger-paint medium with commercial and hand-made tools.

The following chapters in this book include instructions and suggestions for using finger paint as it was originally introduced by Ruth Faison Shaw, and for continuous experiences with tools and mixed media.

All these activities, to be important learning situations, require stimulating teachers who are prepared to present each separate activity. They should know the aims and set up goals for child growth and development through art.

Monoprint of a string design.

Monoprint of a cut paper design.

The Shepherd, monoprint, Victoria Bedford Betts.

Creative Art in Education Clinic, School of Art, Syracuse University, New York.
Photograph, courtesy of Dr. Michael F. Andrews.

Chapter Two
PREPARATION AND PRACTICE

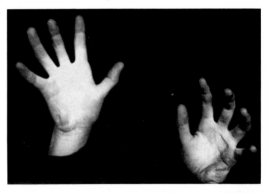

Preparation of the Teacher

Read or review books to understand child development through an understanding of their needs.

Read recent books and magazines about children and art to increase your knowledge.

Read recently written books or articles about artists and art.

See exhibits of work by children and by artists.

Teach to develop all mental powers: absorptive, retentive, reasoning, creative.

Participate in art workshops.

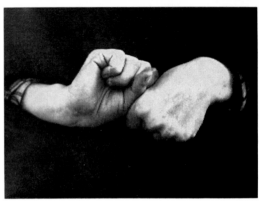

Win a student's confidence and give him freedom to express what he feels through his body, his voice, his hands.

Plan time for motivation, activity, evaluation.

Photographs, courtesy of Philip M. Barclay,
Ardmore Teachers' College,
Papakura, New Zealand.

Teach to guide an inner-discipline by being a shining example, by understanding children, by aiming for better ways of doing things.

Aim to develop esthetic attitudes by well-planned leadership in discussions.

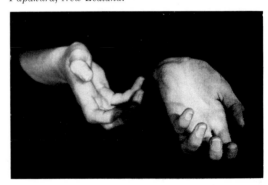

Constantly improve in understanding, in awareness, in enthusiasm, in creative ability.

9

Gladys, Grade 8, William Penn Junior High School,
Fairless Hills, Pennsylvania.
Photograph, courtesy of Doris Kirby, Coordinator of
Art, Pennsbury Schools, Fallsington, Pennsylvania.

Preparation of the Student

Establish confidence with courtesy, consideration, warmth, attention, patience, sincerity, understanding, creative ideas, appreciation.

Find ways of intensifying experiences through sound, motion, literature or vivid descriptions, even when art is tied in with other subjects, to help students re-create images through self-identification.

Expose students to the arts: give them opportunities to create with meaning; learn many things about them; let them learn about you; let them learn about themselves.

Charles M. Boehm High School students visit the Museum of Modern Art. Art Teacher, Marguerite Turner.

Preparation of the Parent

Gain interest and understanding by conference and Parent Teachers Association discussions of the aims and objectives of art experiences: relaxation, enjoyment, creative self-expression, adjustment, enrichment.

Invite parents to attend school art exhibits.

Plan parent and child workshops.

Encourage home exhibits of students' work. Remind parents that appliances, mirrors, varnished or enameled wood are not damaged by gummed tape.

Continue parent interest and participation by sending home bulletins or friendly letters written by students or teachers. Supply information about school and community art activities. Request discarded and scrap materials needed for future activities.

Spring Festival, Williamsport, Pennsylvania. Photograph, courtesy of Eva L. Keller, who, as Supervisor of Art for eighteen years, introduced finger painting to all grades and to parents.

Photograph, courtesy of Ruth Flurry, Atlanta, Georgia.

Grade 1, Liberty Street School, Middletown, New York.
Photographs, courtesy of Sylvia A. Wruck, Gasport,
New York.
Special finger paint tray, courtesy of the Park Studio,
101 Wickham Avenue, Middletown, New York.

Preparation for Painting

Working areas	—classrooms, art room, cafeteria, gymnasium, hallways.
Working surfaces	—smooth, flat, washable surfaces.
Working materials	—grouped in accessible areas and near a source or supply of water.
Drying areas	—in or on racks, under desks or tables, on desks, on chairs, over backs of chairs, in cardboard trays which can be stacked.
Paint storage	—shelves, cartons.
Paper storage	—shelves, cartons, portfolios, market bags.
Smock storage	—coat closets, lockers, cartons.
Pans and buckets	—store them, full of sponges and cloths, in closets or on low shelves.
Newspapers	—store few; collect more when needed.
Empty containers	—nest cans, cups and cartons to save space.
Tools	—store in labeled boxes; include directions for the care of tools.

Suggestions

Enlist the cooperation of principal, teachers, custodians and parents in providing space or equipment for large painting activities. When an art room or cafeteria is not available, trade rooms with a kindergarten teacher. Use boards or sturdy blocks to raise the tables to a desired height.

Encourage continued cooperation by leaving working areas neat and clean.

Let the children be helpers, even in expressing their appreciation.

Photographs, courtesy of Sylvia A. Wruck.

Motivation

In considering any suggestion for stimulating students, remember that the motivation should be introduced in terms of personal feelings and experiences. Originality and imagination mean a personal new way of expression. Materials are important and can be a strong motivation, but they need the accompanying stimulus of personal involvement.

Photograph, courtesy of Philip M. Barclay, Ardmore Teachers' College, Papakura, New Zealand.

Suggestions

Direct, purposeful experiences
Contrived experiences
Dramatization
Demonstrations
Field trips
Exhibitions
Films and television
Still pictures
Visual symbols
Verbal symbols

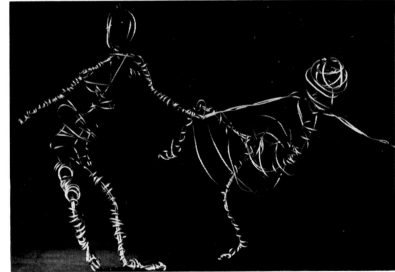

13

New learnings affect and change previous ones. The mingling of new and old will be done by the student. His knowledge will be applied when specific needs arise and applied *then* in relation to his ability.

Motivation materials and suggestions can vary with school systems, with building locations, even with groups within a classroom.

Photograph, courtesy of Mrs. Robert Booke, Brooklyn, New York.

Grade 6, Lyndover School, Teacher, Jessyln Meyers. Photograph, courtesy of Pauline Medlen, Art Director, Maplewood-Richmond Heights Schools, Missouri.

Demonstration

Presentations of techniques or skills should involve recognition of students' problems, expressions of possible solutions, information and materials for solutions and encouragement during the work period.

Think about the age, the need and the interest when planning a demonstration. It can be a valuable experience if it is well planned and well carried out.

Establish rapport: let students participate and appreciate good suggestions from them.

Hold attention: handle materials efficiently; introduce variety; provide for participation.

Establish readiness: be familiar with earlier experiences; explain vocabulary; introduce motivating questions.

Provide for individual differences: group slow and fast learners; use fact questions for slow learners and thought questions for fast ones.

Tie the lesson together: provide for retention of facts; use facts to stimulate critical thinking.

Provide for follow-up experiences, for individual participation and for research.

Present techniques, when needed, as means to aid self-expression.

Remember that good demonstrations can translate theory into practice.

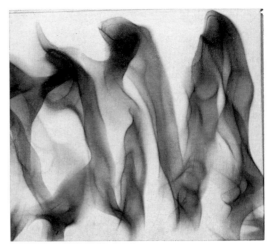

Smoke Painting, Granite School District, Salt Lake City, Utah.
Photograph, courtesy of Delbert W. Smedley, Supervisor of Art, and Daniel W. Brown, Grade 6 Teacher, Sherman School.

Mass, space and color.
Photograph, courtesy of Alma E. McConnell, Instructor in Art Education, San Francisco State College, California.

Susan, Age 8, Yardley, Pennsylvania.

Chapter Three
FINGER PAINTING

Finger painting is popular with both children and adults. Tiny tots enjoy the feel of the paint and the opportunity to swing freely, unhampered by tools. Many make up stories to tell. In later years they integrate thought and painting with writing, spelling and English.

Throughout the grades and with adults, the medium can be explored for art, education and recreation. As a medium for therapy, finger paint is used in guidance, psycho-analysis, occupational therapy, sight-saving and other branches of work for the mentally and physically handicapped. In all fields of usage, an experienced and trained teacher is essential.

Danny, Age 2.
Photograph, courtesy of Anna Dunser,
Richmond Heights, Missouri.

Approach

No medium should be approached with limited vision. Finger painting can be a mud pie for the very young or for those of any age who need mud-pie making. It can be a gymnasium for a would-be athlete, an instrument for musical interpretation, a record for the psychiatrist or a new means of expression for the student and artist.

Different ages and different individuals respond to finger painting in different ways. With all, creative expression is prompted from within by a reaction to a stimulant.

How does one teach finger painting? One starts with the needs of the students, with familiarity with the medium, and with enthusiasm.

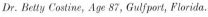

Dr. Betty Costine, Age 87, Gulfport, Florida.

Essential Materials

Moist finger paint   —a thick, ready-to-use paint which is harmless to skin and clothing. Available in red, blue, yellow, orange, green, violet, brown, black and white.*

Dry finger paint   —a powder which can be mixed with water to make a moist finger paint, or sprinkled and mixed directly on a wet paper.

Donald, Grade 1, Washington School, Nutley, New Jersey.
Photograph, courtesy of Evelyn K. Corso, Supervisor of Art.

Finger-paint paper   —a special washable glazed paper, or any paper that can be rubbed with water without destroying the surface. Paper should be large enough to permit free swinging motions and a repeat of hand and arm impressions. Special white finger-paint paper is available in 16″ x 11″ and 16″ x 22″.

Working surface   —any smooth, flat, washable surface, approximately waist high.

Kyle, Age 6, Makefield School, Yardley, Pennsylvania.

Paper pan   —larger than the paper in use, for wetting the sheet completely.

Water pan   —to provide water during the painting process.

Large sponge   —to wet the paper completely when a pan is not available.

*For paint and paper information, please write to your school supply dealer.

18

Pencil or crayon	—to record the date, to identify the owner of the painting and the dull side of the paper. Both sides look glazed when the paper is wet.

Elaine, Grade 6, Manhasset, Long Island, New York.

Spatulas or spoons	—to serve the paint, from the container to the paper or from paint jar to individual containers.
Buckets	—to wash hands, sponges, paint rags and table.
Sponges or cloths	—to clean hands and working surfaces.
Newspapers or cardboards	—to dry wet paintings and to press dry paintings. Wrinkles in dry paintings can be pressed with a warm iron or under weights.
Aprons, smocks, or old shirts	—to protect clothing.

Douglas, Age 12, Ho-Ho-Kus, New Jersey.

Jan, Grade 1, Village Park School,
Fairless Hills, Pennsylvania.
Art Teacher, Karl Schantz.

19

Motivation Suggestions for Beginners

A short, simple demonstration to show the process of wetting the paper, smoothing and spreading the paint and experimenting with hands and arms.

A dry run demonstration when time is limited or when only a review of the process is needed.

A film of the process, followed by a brief discussion.*

Photographs or sketches of the process used with or without an opaque projector, depending on the size of the group.

Discussions of the parts of the hand and arm with students participating in a dry run demonstration of motions in the air or on desks.

An exhibit of children's finger paintings followed by a brief demonstration.

The Process

Prepare materials and equipment. Place them near a sink or water bucket.

Improve working and watching space by re-arranging tables or desks.

Decide on the size of the painting group. Provide sufficient space for each student.

Discuss the distribution plan for paint, paper and water before the activity begins.

Discuss posture and a preferred standing position, when possible, to permit freedom of movement.

*"Sea Adventures of Sandy the Snail", Artist, Betty Ohlrogge Dabbs, Encyclopaedia-Britannica Films, 1150 Wilmette Avenue, Wilmette, Illinois.

Examine the paper and write name and date on the dull side.

Wet the paper completely in a pan of water or with a wet sponge.

Smooth the wet paper on a table so that no wrinkles or air bubbles are visible. Leave a wide border of table surface around the paper to provide swinging space and room for excess paint.

Place a heaping teaspoonful on the paper and spread it smoothly over the entire sheet. Add water and mix it well so that the paint will be obedient to motions and impressions.

Enjoy the feeling of moving the paint with any and all parts of your hand or arm. As you practice, remember to keep the paint obedient by mixing water with it while you work. Just rub the paint smooth to erase rejected motions and continue to explore.

When a discovery pleases you so much that you want to keep it, pick up the paper by two corners and place it on newspapers to dry.

Scrape excess paint on the table into a spare container to use for other paintings.

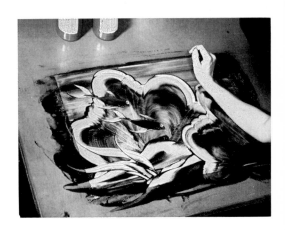

Always clean hands, arms, table and equipment before starting another painting.

If paint gets on cotton clothing, soak it first in cold water, then wash it in warm soap suds. Let paint dry on woolens, then brush it off with a clean bristle.

THE HAND
IS MAN'S MOST
VERSATILE TOOL

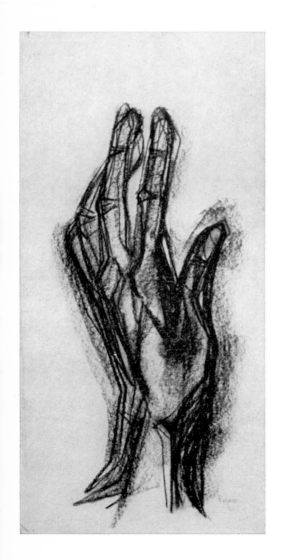

Tools for Finger Painting

Whole hand —flat and relaxed.

Flat palm —fingers raised.

Side of hand —fingers extended straight.

Side of hand —fingers curved.

Clenched fist —thumb up.

Outer side of thumb —fingers raised.

Base of thumb —fingers raised.

Base of palm —rest of hand raised.

Knuckles —in different positions.

Flat part of finger or fingers relaxed.

Finger tips —both ball and side of tip.

Thumb —ball and side of thumb tip.

Fingernails —use lightly to avoid paper tears.

Whole arm including wrist relaxed.

Fleshy part of arm —with wrist and elbow raised.

Elbow

Man-made —accept any tool that the student introduces on his own during the painting activity.

Sketch by Ann Franco Ferreira, Doylestown, Pennsylvania.

Experiment with Impressions and Motions

Pat, touch and lift.

Swing, shove, push, stroke, wiggle, zig-zag, scallop, circle, spiral.

Try all parts of the hand and arm; use both hands or both arms at the same time.

Repeat a discovery to help you remember it.

Notice the textures and differences in each experiment.

Enjoy a paint that permits trial and error, which may show a way to something new or better.

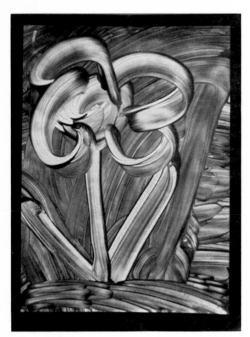

*Patricia, Kindergarten, Makefield School,
Yardley, Pennsylvania.*

*Diane, Grade 5, Makefield School.
Art teacher, Ann F. Thompson.*

Experiment with Value

Work with one color for freedom of movement.

Learn to control dark and light areas by pressure and by paint color or consistency:

> Use less paint, white paint or more water to lighten a color.

> Use more paint, black paint or less water to darken a color.

Use a swiping motion to pick up excess paint on the table. Add it to the painting with a gentle pat or stroke.

Experiment with Color

Mix two colors together while spreading the paint on the paper. Remember to use less of each color than the teaspoonful suggested for work with one ready-mixed color.

Spread different paint colors in separate areas of the paper. Blend the colors by sweeping one into another with a light pressure.

Mix colors on the table when a new color is to be added on a small area of a painting.

For controlled areas of new colors, remove the background paint from the areas with cloth or sponge. Clean your hand before picking up a new color which has been rubbed smooth on the table. Add new colors with a gentle touch.

For multicolored paintings, reserve room on the working surface for a palette of colors which have been rubbed smooth and mixed with water.

For multicolored paintings, work quickly while the paint is wet. Mix background paint and table palette of colors to the same consistency.

24

Variety in Working Surfaces

Varnished wood	Enameled wood
Linoleum	Formica, or varnished masonite
Vinyl	Adhesive-backed plastic
Oil cloth	Fabric-backed plastic
Porcelain	Glass, marble or metal

Any smooth, flat, washable surface, large enough for the paper size selected and for the planned activity.

Variety in Painting Surfaces

Glazed, washable papers in white or colors —finger-paint paper, washable shelf paper, butcher paper, freezer paper, bakery bag paper, bristol board, book or magazine stock, oaktag, Fadeless papers.*

Unglazed, washable papers —wallpaper, water-color paper, canvas board.

Transparent papers —parchment, tracing.

Decorative washable papers —metallic paper, textured paper.

Susan, Age 6, and Tommy, Age 9, paint at home. Photograph, courtesy of Wilma Geer Bradbury, Falmouth Foreside, Maine.

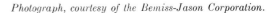

Photograph, courtesy of the Bemiss-Jason Corporation.

*For information about eighteen colors of Fadeless papers, please write to the Bemiss-Jason Corporation, 3250 Ash Street, Palo Alto, California, or 49–20 Van Dam Street, Long Island City, New York.

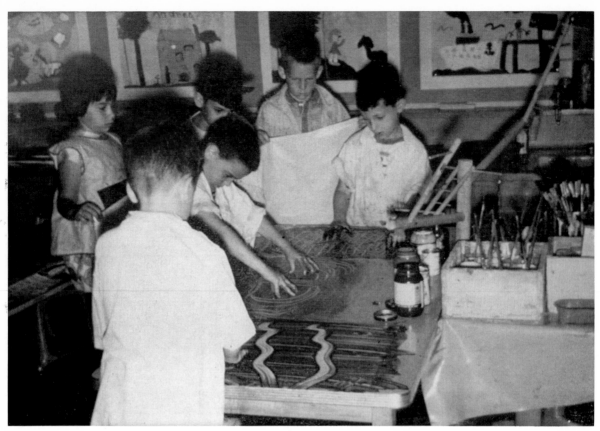

We take turns and learn by watching.

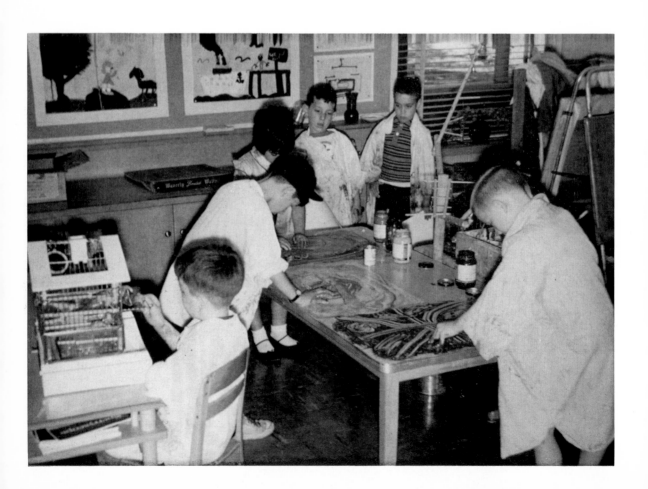

We clean up and tell Mrs. Lowe about our paintings.

Grade 1, Clover Drive School, Great Neck, Long Island, New York.
Photographs, courtesy of the teacher, Ethel Black Lowe.

Ray, Age 4.

Kindergarten, Makefield School,
Yardley, Pennsylvania.

Susan, Age 5.

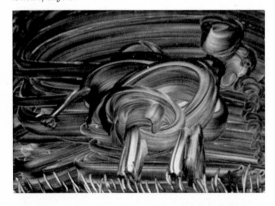

Ricky, Age 5.

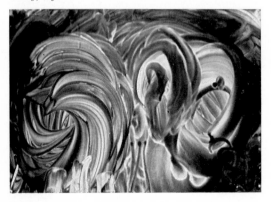

Variety in Experiments

"Play" or get acquainted with the feeling of the paint and with motion. Work with one color, but let it be a free color choice.

"Play," with free choice of colors; learn new motions and new parts of the hand; develop an awareness of contrast.

Paint to music; dance with the hands in wet paint.

Paint after listening to music; this suggestion is for older or more sensitive students.

Paint after telling, hearing or reading a story or poem.

Paint after a field trip; have a discussion of highlights of the trip before the actual painting experience.

Paint all-over or border designs after a discussion of possible uses for paper crafts.

Feel textures; discuss differences; provide a follow-up opportunity to paint rough and smooth "feelings" in paint.

Fold a wet painting of one or more colors. Try fold-overs in any direction: vertical, horizontal, diagonal.

Fold a wet finger painting. Try vigorous motions on the top of the fold-over.

Fold a wet finger painting and pull or drag the top section over the paint as the sheet is unfolded. Try several colors of paint in a second experiment. Fold-overs aid muscular coordination.

Paint after a discussion of new perspectives: imagine views looking down from high places; pretend you are a tiny insect looking around you.

Use a magnifying glass or a microscope to offer new perspectives.

Paint after a discussion of weather or season: a windy day, a rainy night, a sunny spring day.

Plan time for the dramatization of a story or poem before a painting experience.

Introduce smells or sounds as motivation. Ask the children to close their eyes while using noses and ears. Plan time for verbal expression before the painting begins.

Paint after a brief discussion and evaluation of an exhibit of earlier finger-painting experiences.

Paint distance by doing the background and far-away things first and the close-up things last. Discuss other possible ways of achieving distance.

Paint after a brief discussion of a selected topic familiar to the students.

Discuss plans for original story-book illustrations.

Paint after a classroom exhibit and discussion of natural materials, collected by the students.

Paint after showing a film which has been pre-viewed by the teacher.

Present and discuss papers of different sizes, shapes and colors; follow by free choice of paper in the painting experience.

Present mats of different sizes and shapes and cardboard strips to frame a selected section of a dry painting; follow with a mat-making activity.

Present a variety of colors and textures of papers and cardboard on which to mount paintings. Discuss paste, tape, staples. Let the student select his finger painting to mount on a backing.

Grade 5, Laboratory School, University of Chicago, Illinois.
Photographs, courtesy of Jessie Todd, Art Teacher.

Grade 6, Program Cover.
Photograph, courtesy of Anna Dunser, Richmond Heights, Missouri.

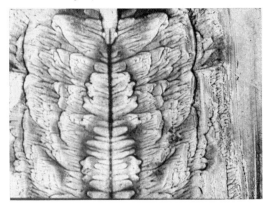

29

Dragon, Age 11, Emerson, New Jersey Schools.

Suggestions

Encourage students to respond verbally and freely.

Teach to simplify or clarify a personal experience.

Compare new materials and tools with familiar ones, in discussions and in demonstrations.

Talk about their differences.

Present different ways of using each material.

Offer variety in paper sizes and colors.

Supply motivation when it is needed.

Help children to solve their own problems.

Guide students to develop their paintings.

Accept a refusal in an assigned topic.

Establish good habits in art activities.

Record each child's development through art. Make notes of attitudes and progress during or soon after each activity.

Pussy Willows, Age 13, Emerson, New Jersey Schools.

Photographs, courtesy of Muriel Ray, Supervisor of Art, Emerson, New Jersey.

30

Portrait, High School, Hammond, Indiana.
Photograph, courtesy of Olga Schubkagel,
Supervisor of Art.

Falling Water, Veronica, High School, Ely, Minnesota.
Photograph, courtesy of Frances Stokes Pulley,
Cameron, Missouri.

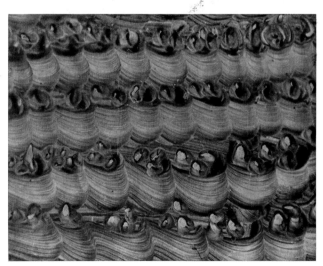

A Night at the Opera, Harold, Age 16,
Cliffside Heights, New Jersey.

Grade 6, Lyndover School, Maplewood-Richmond Heights Schools, Missouri.
Photograph, courtesy of Pauline Medlen, Art Director.

Chapter Four
MONOPRINTS

No medium should restrict a student to one method of expression or to special or limited tools. Possibilities must be explored to learn and understand reasons for possible limitations. Discoveries need not all be known or found by one individual. They can be gained by observing more experienced students and teachers, by watching others work and by solving problems—alone and with help.

Monoprints are transfers of paintings made on finger-paint paper or on smooth working surfaces. Although several prints can be made of one painting, one varies from another. There are many ways of transferring a design. Classifications can help to clarify the processes.

Harry, Age 5, Makefield School, Yardley, Pennsylvania.

Essential Materials and Equipment

Finger paint
Water and cleaning equipment
Papers for prints —papers for finger painting,* unprinted newspaper, manila, construction, bogus, charcoal, water-color, oaktag, brown wrapping, canvas boards, novelty papers, wallpapers, newspaper and magazine pages, paper towels, white and colored gift tissue, hand decorated papers, smooth and textured boards.

*Please refer to the complete list in Chapter Three, page 25.

Grade 6, Lyndover School.

Fabrics for prints —glazed chintz, polished cotton, any firmly woven fabric; wool, felt, burlap, novelty weaves with body.

Optional Materials

String	Paper or plastic lace
Confetti	Cut or torn papers
Toothpicks	Textured fabrics
Leaves	Textured rubber
Grasses	Textured plastics
Straws	Flat flowers
Sawdust	Oil-based clay
Spaghetti	Novelty tapes

Transfer Tools

Squeegees or scrapers —cardboard, beveled wood, rubber, plastic, metal, felt, thumb, side of hand, arm.

Brayers —rubber, wood, cardboard, sponge rollers, tin cans covered with felt, rubber or sponge cloth.

Stylus —pencil, orange stick, crochet hook, any dull-pointed tool.

Blocks —rubber, wood, sponge, cardboard.

Natural materials —leaves, grasses, pressed flowers.

Brushes —soft and stiff, pointed and flat, discarded toothbrushes.

Palettes —table surface, waxed paper, cookie tin, any smooth washable surface.

Lifted Monoprints

Process

Make a finger painting on glazed paper or on a smooth table.

Place any kind of paper to be printed on top of the wet finger painting.

Rub gently over the back of the printing paper using the hand, a scraper or a brayer.

Lift the print.   Observe a reverse transfer.

Make a second print in the same way, but use more pressure on the transfer tool since there is less paint to lift.

Lift a third print on a wet printing paper.

Age 14, Emerson, New Jersey Schools.
Photograph, courtesy of Muriel Ray,
Supervisor of Art.

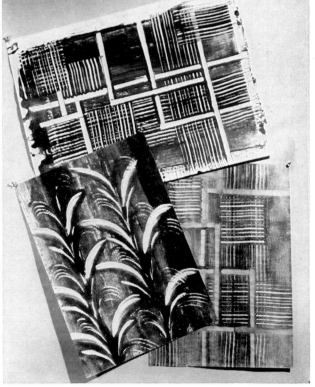

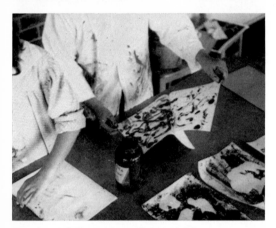

David and CiCi, Grade 5, Makefield School, Yardley, Pennsylvania.
Photographs, courtesy of Dr. Henry Ray.

Experiment with Materials

Arrange wet or dry string on a wet finger painting. Cover with printing paper, rub and peel off a print.

Remove the string. Make a different second print.

Color string with paint before creating a design. Plan contrast when selecting paint colors for string and for the finger painting.

Crayon free line designs on dry paper before making a finger painting. Use the lines as guides for string designs or for hand motions.

Work with cut or torn papers; overlap some, if you wish, as you place them on the wet paint.

After making a print, use the paint-covered papers as stamping tools to make a different print on a dry, clean paper.

Combine string with paper to block out areas in a finger painting before making a lifted monoprint.

Megan, Grade 5, Makefield School.

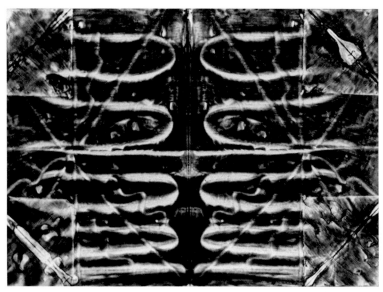

Photograph, courtesy of Dr. John Lembach,
Acting Head, Department of Art,
University of Maryland, College Park.

Lift a print of blots of paint. Add blots of another color and repeat the process on the same printing paper. Print one color at a time. Use as many colors as you wish.

Design with leaves, grasses and other flat natural materials. Arrange them on a wet painting; lift one or more prints.

Explore many kinds, sizes and shapes of printing papers and fabrics.

Lift prints on thin wood, cork and styrofoam.

Try very wet finger paint and a tacky paint. Discover how the paint consistency affects prints on smooth or rough, glazed or absorbent, thin or thick, printing materials.

Employ the lifted monoprint process in transferring wet prints made by other processes presented in this chapter and in the two following chapters.

Bonnie, Grade 4, Makefield School.
Art Teacher, Ann F. Thompson.
Photographs, courtesy of Dr. Henry Ray.

CiCi and David, Grade 5, Makefield School.

Tooled Lifted Prints

Process

Spread tacky finger paint on a table or on a dry paper.

Place a printing paper on the finger painting.

Rub your hand over it with gentle touch.

With a stylus make a picture or pattern on the back of the printing paper.

Lift a print. Observe a reverse transfer.

Lift a second print of the tooled impression in the paint on the table. Add more stylus strokes, if you wish, before lifting the second print.

Experiment

Try rolling a brayer over the paint before covering it with a printing paper. Use tacky finger paint for a textured background that resembles a wood grain. Let wet paint dry on the table until it is tacky.

Use brushes, feathers, combs, sponges, finger or hand and arm pats for different textures in tacky finger paint. Apply a printing paper over the paint texture; rub over it gently with your hand before tooling a design on the back of the printing paper.

Simplify the clean-up process by first folding a sheet of paper in half. Smooth finger paint on one side of the opened fold; add texture to the paint; fold the paper together and use a stylus on top of the folder. Open the sheet to dry the two prints.

Explore all kinds of papers for graphic prints. Discover the tools best for smooth papers and those best for clear prints on rough papers.

Plan areas of different colors or of blended colors in the paint textures created with hand or commercial tools.

Extend and control detailed or precise work with a pointed tool by making a preliminary pencil sketch on the back of the printing paper. Do this before the paper is placed on a paint texture.

Feel free to add ink, crayon or paint accents or definitions on a dry print.

Graphic designs by Rosemarie Mandarino.

39

Scraped Monoprints

Process

Review the list of optional materials.

Design with one or more dry or wet materials on a clean wet or dry paper or on a smooth or textured working surface. For a permanent arrangement, glue the materials on a strong paper or on a board. Add a taut cover of very thin plastic when materials are affected by moisture.

Cover the composition of materials with a wet finger-paint paper. Eliminate bubbles and wrinkles.

Spread finger paint over the entire sheet.

With a squeegee or scraper of cardboard, wood or rubber, scrape over the paint to make a print of the raised materials under the paper. Continue to scrape until the print is satisfactory.

Lift the print; clean the table of paint; cover the raised materials with a second sheet of wet paper and paint. Continue to make scraped prints using different colors or blended colors.

Notice that scraped prints are not reversed.

Experiment with Scraping Strokes

Use light and strong pressures to produce differences in the prints.

Try vertical, horizontal and diagonal strokes of the scraping tool.

Scrape with short or long strokes, with smooth or broken strokes.

Experiment with Materials

Sandwich leaves between two pieces of waxed paper and press with a hot iron to seal the leaves in a planned position. Sandwich other flat materials in the same way to make a permanent arrangement for scraped prints.

Cover stitchery with Saran Wrap or any thin plastic taped taut to a cardboard or table base. This will protect the stitchery from moisture and paint.

Use a textured working surface for variety in background when designing with raised materials.

Make cut-outs of textured papers or fabrics to arrange on a smooth working surface.

Collect dividers from gift or display cartons. Open them flat, cut them apart and use the sections to create original designs.

Use carved linoleum or wood under wet finger paint paper for scraped prints.

Additional materials and methods for creating raised designs are: drippings of wax, cement, or thick paint on paper or cardboard; string or rubber bands woven around a cardboard; string woven to pins or tacks that border a cardboard; thin uncooked spaghetti, or cooked spaghetti arranged on a paper working surface while still wet and allowed to dry. Design with strands of oil-based clay, or recessed impressions in a sheet of clay.

Experiment with Color

Use a table palette of smooth paint as a source from which to pick up color with a brayer or a scraper.

Spread separate colors on sections of the wet finger-paint paper before scraping.

41

Linda, Age 5, Makefield School,
Yardley, Pennsylvania.

New Jersey School for the Deaf, Trenton.
Art Director, Helene C. Condon.

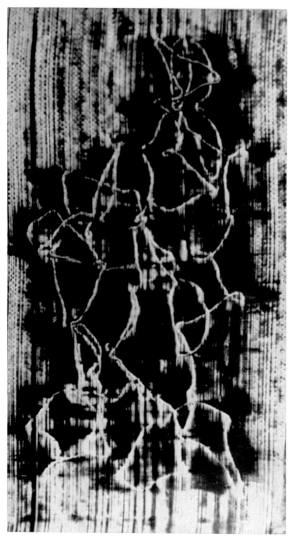

Central High School, Trenton, New Jersey.
Art Teacher, Daphne Koenig.

*Prints by Eleanor J. Young,
Lebanon, New Jersey.*

*Henry Ahrens, guest consultant, discusses
activities with a workshop member.*

*Creative Art Education Workshop, Rutgers
University S. S., New Brunswick, New Jersey.
Photographs, courtesy of Marion Quin Dix,
Director of Art Education, Elizabeth, New
Jersey Schools.*

*Mask, Carol Anthes,
Port Angeles, Washington.*

44

Photograph, courtesy of Dr. John Lembach,
Acting Head, Department of Art,
University of Maryland, College Park.

Pulled Prints

Process

Spread very wet finger paint on a table or on a sheet of finger-paint paper. Use any motion of the hand or arm.

Place a clean wet sheet of paper, glazed side down, on top of the wet paint and pull it off with gentle or vigorous motions.

Experiment

Change direction as you pull or drag the top sheet over the bottom one.

Arrange string or cut paper on the wet finger painting before covering and pulling the top sheet.

Blend colors on the finger painting before pulling a print.

Use a wet pulled print as a background for hand or tool foreground motions.

Let dry pulled prints whet imagination. Add crayon, paint or cut paper to develop a print and to show your selection of important lines or shapes.

Boy, Age 12, Emerson, New Jersey Schools.
Art Supervisor, Muriel Ray.

45

Creative Art in Education Clinic, School of Art,
Syracuse University, New York.
Photographs, courtesy of Dr. Michael F. Andrews.

Chapter Five
PAINTING WITH TOOLS

"What counts in a painting is not whether or not a particular tool is used but rather, how that tool is used! Any tool that serves a particular esthetic intention or series of intentions is the right tool to use."*

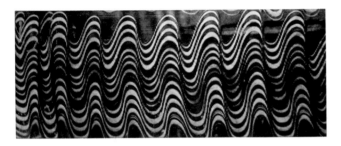

All available resources should be used to make experiences vital. Painting tool collections can be a treasure chest for all teachers and children in a school building. Adults can start the collections by showing a few in use, or by discussing them. Children can enlarge the collections and can organize the tools for many and varied painting activities.

While working they will discover the unique characteristics of finger paint: how to use it thick and thin, and how record both fine and bold textures of tool strokes or impressions.

Good judgment must be used by the teacher. Too many tools can overstimulate or confuse students. When possible, appropriate ones for immediate needs can be selected by the teacher from the collection and made available to the students.

*Burt Wasserman, *School Arts Magazine*, October, 1961.

Central High School, Trenton, New Jersey.
Art Teacher, Daphne Koenig.

Essential Materials

Finger paint
Variety in paper
Accessible water and cleaning equipment
Available tools and adequate space

Painting Tools

Brushes	—of all sizes and shapes: soft hair, bristles, even worn ones. Eyelash, toothbrushes, nail brushes, pastry brushes. Spurn none.
Cardboard	—of different thicknesses and sizes, corrugated and other strong, textured boards, drinking straws.
Natural materials	—twigs, feathers, weeds, moss, bark, pieces of fruits or vegetables.

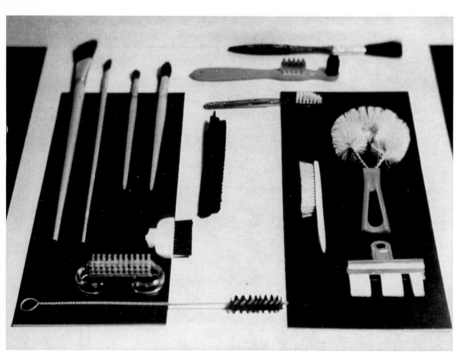

Wood	—chips, scrap wedges, block edges, beveled molding, toothpicks, original shapes modeled of plastic wood, large and toy rolling pins, dowels, clothespins, door knobs, assorted scrap forms.

Photograph, courtesy of Dr. John Lembach,
Acting Head, Department of Art,
University of Maryland, College Park.

Rubber	—pieces of inner tubes, window wedges, furniture casters, brayers, hair curlers, plate scrapers, windshield wipers, squeegees, rubber heels, covered wire, original ones of cement, balls, rubber bands.
Felt	—pieces of old hats or slippers, sturdy scraps.
Sponge	—scrap pieces, paint rollers, hair curlers, old place mats, corn and bunion plasters.
Plastic	—hard or soft vinyl scraps, mats, containers, combs.
Fibers	—cord, rope, cork, rug scraps, fabric pads held by hands or attached to handles.

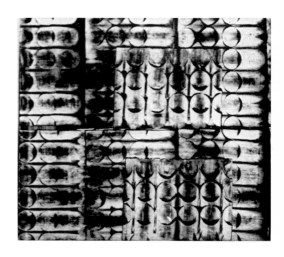

Experiment with Brushes

Easel paintings —use a bristle brush. Notice that the paint is dripless when no water is added. Wipe the brush on a damp cloth before using a different color. Clean-up is quick and easy.

Transparent paintings —use pointed or flat soft brushes. Dilute finger paint with water, on the brush or premix it in a pan or on a palette. Do not imitate water-color work, but discover the qualities of finger paint.

Opaque paintings —try undiluted paint with soft brushes. Try building up paint layers or applying a second coat on dry paint. Discover characteristics of the finger-paint medium.

Spatter painting —use stiff brushes against a spatula or screen to spatter paint for texture or to paint a background around flat shapes or string designs arranged on any paper or fabric.

Sponge painting —try different kinds of sponges for texture or to dab paint around flat shapes on a paper. Cut them for needed sizes and shapes.

Patty, Grade 4, Brookview School, Morrisville, Pennsylvania. Art Teacher, Ann F. Thompson.

50

Stencil painting —cut designs in water resistant papers or in absorbent ones. Save positive and negative stencil sections (positive stencil—a shape cut out of paper; negative stencil—the paper from which the positive shape has been cut). Use them for planned designs on paper, wood, walls or fabrics. With spatter or sponge, add color to the surface area not protected by a stencil. Notice that undiluted finger paint has body and does not bleed or run. Use less finger paint for transparent color when overlapping is desired. Explore tools other than sponge or brush, for stencil work. Discuss safety rules before sharp tools are offered for stencil cutting.

—Control the paint for small stencil use, by first patting it near the edge of the stencil; use a clean tool to move the paint from the stencil edge to the painting paper.

—For some spatter work with stiff brushes and stencils, first thin finger paint on the table, on a palette of waxed paper, or on a coated magazine page.

Grade 6, Lyndover School, Maplewood-Richmond Heights Schools, Missouri. Art Director, Pauline Medlen.

51

Print by Arlene Mondoruza.

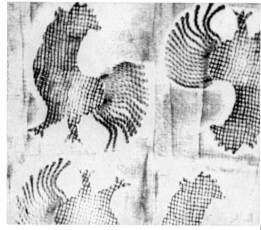

Print by Florence Nowland.
Photographs, courtesy of Dr. L. John G. Wenner,
Fine Arts Department, Central Connecticut State
College, New Britain.

Experiment with Brayers

Roll a brayer of cardboard, wood or rubber directly on a wet finger painting.

Roll the brayer first in a color rubbed smooth on a table top, then over a wet painting.

Roll the brayer over wet confetti, string, etc., then over a wet finger painting. Observe the resulting textures.

Use string or cut paper to block out lines and shapes in sections of a wet paper. Roll over the arrangement with paint.

Use leaves and grasses instead of string and paper for arrangements.

Explore designing with other materials on a wet finger painting.

Plan ample space for a table palette when many colors will be used for brayer painting.

Use brayer and table palette for work on clean dry textured papers or fabrics.

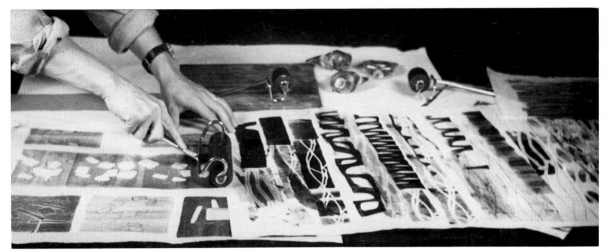

Explore thin and thick paint on a brayer. Think about your reaction to each consistency and the reaction of the tool.

Combine various techniques in one painting.

Combine colors on a brayer. Discover ways to control color areas on paper.

Arrange flat materials, either smooth or textured, under a wet finger painting. Roll over the paint to record an impression of the arrangement.

Combine brayer painting with brush work or with strokes of other tools.

Photograph, courtesy of Bailey Films, Inc., and Reino Randall, Associate Professor of Art, Central Washington State College, Ellensburg, Washington.

Photograph, courtesy of Dr. John Lembach, Acting Head, Department of Art, University of Maryland, College Park.

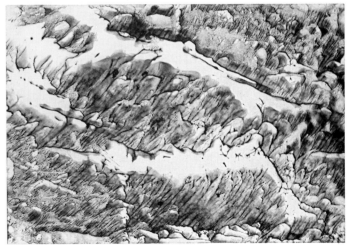

Photograph, courtesy of Elizabeth C. Wynkoop, Trenton, New Jersey.

Experiment with Cardboard

Collect cardboards; tape an edge for strength; notch an edge for variety. Save cardboards of various widths and thicknesses.

On a wet finger painting, make practice strokes with the cardboard scraps. Try light and heavy pressure.

Vary the length, direction and movement of strokes. Discover ways of obtaining texture.

Pretend the tool is the side of your hand as you move or pat it in the paint.

Blend or mix colors of finger paint before using the edge or part of the flat side of cardboard for strokes.

Extend the tool's use by using it as a palette knife. Smooth paint colors on a table palette; pick up each color with a clean cardboard or wipe a single tool clean between colors.

Use a strong paper with a tooth when paint is applied in layers.

Practice lettering with a cardboard tool.

Work with cardboard tools on dry, rough papers.

Boy, Age 14, Emerson, New Jersey Schools.
Supervisor of Art, Muriel Ray.

Painting by Maryln Cadwell.
Photograph, courtesy of Dr. L. John G. Wenner.

Victoria Bedford Betts.

Experiment with String

Collect string, cord, rope, raffia, of different lengths. Cut some short and bunch them to resemble a brush. Knot other pieces together for a different tool.

"Play" with string tools on wet finger paint. Repeat strokes to remember them.

Fold a wet finger painting in half. Open and arrange clean strings on one side. Fold again, rub over the top of the folder; open and remove strings. Try this with two separate papers.

Try paint-covered string for other experiments; use them on clean dry paper or on wet paintings.

With either clean or paint-covered strings, make an arrangement on one half of the open finger painting; let one end of each string trail off the paper edge. Fold the paper, add weights to anchor the strings, then pull them out.

For another trial, arrange strings over the entire painting; let one end of each string trail off the paper. Cover the painting and strings with a clean sheet of dry paper; add weights and pull out each string.

Experiment for Continuous Learning

Collect scraps of rubber, felt, plastics, soft wood;
use them as painting tools. Cut them to fit your
needs.

Explore natural materials for painting tools.
Some fruits and vegetables can be sliced or notched
for firm tools; others have foliage that can be
flexible tools.

Natural or synthetic sponges can be utilized for
large work or can be cut up and held by a clip
when a small tool is needed. Sponge tools can be
combined with brushes for different effects in the
same painting.

Be on the look-out for new materials that can be
utilized as tools for painting or printing.

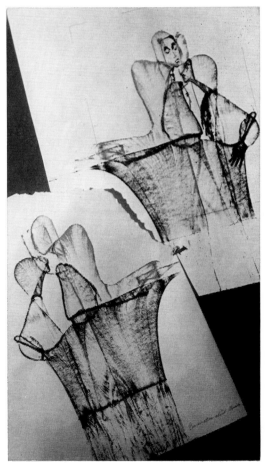

Creative Art in Education Clinic,
School of Art, Syracuse University, New York.
Photographs, courtesy of Dr. Michael F. Andrews.

Chapter Six

PRINTING WITH TOOLS

"Only that day dawns to which we are awake."*

There are countless source-adventures related to tool collecting. Interest can be retained by actual use of tools, through demonstrations and exhibits.

Familiarity with a wide range of materials can lead students to extend their use to printing explorations.

Impressions of tools are simply records of touch and lift motions. Prints can be pats of a finger tip on paint or impressions of complex designs created with materials.

Review essential materials and painting tools listed in the preceding chapter. Discuss additional materials which can be used as tools or utilized for making raised designs on blocks or rollers. Discuss tools and processes for raising or for recessing designs in a block or a roller.

Essential Materials for Tools

Blocks	—sponge, wood, cardboard, rubber, plastic, stone.
Rollers	—cardboard, sponge, rubber, fabric, wood, metal, stone.

*Henry David Thoreau.

59

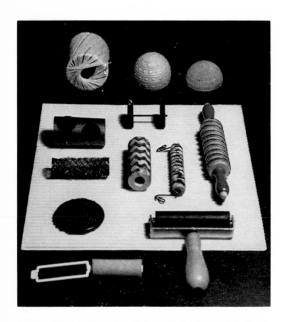

Bird in Hand, Dorothea Schnepf.

Age 13, Emerson, New Jersey Schools.
Supervisor of Art, Muriel Ray.

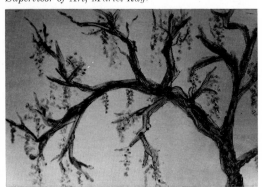

Optional Materials for Tools

Paper	—of various weights and textures.
Textured fabric	—burlap, monk's cloth, rug scraps, novelty tapes and laces, stitchery.
Nonhardening oil clay	—solid blocks, clay-filled box or jar lids, clay covering on cans, dowels or blocks, balls of clay.
Natural materials	—fruits and vegetables, weeds, stones, shells.
Miscellaneous	—linoleum, putty, weather stripping, adhesive tape, cork, cement, wax.

Cutting and Carving Tools

Scissors	Penpoints	Knives
Blades	Gouges	Files

Paint Transfer Tools

Finger	Sponge	Brayer
Brush	Fabric	Cardboard

Print Transfer Tools

Hand	Brayer	Jar bottom
Spoon	Squeegee	Padded hammer

Clay Tools

Commercial tools	Smooth sticks	Hairpins

Personal Tools

Any part of your fingers, hand or arm.

Adhesives

Paste	—paper, cloth, cardboard. School paste is not waterproof.
*Polyvinyl resin glue**	—paper, wood, fabric, all porous materials. Strong, versatile, not waterproof.
Household cement	—paper, wood, leather, metal, glass. Strong, clear, waterproof.
Plastic cement	—paper, wood, glass, metal, most common plastics. Waterproof.
Rubber cement	—paper, fabric, cork, rubber. Strong, not clear, waterproof.

Process

Invent printing tools. Create raised designs by adhering any material to stamping blocks or on rollers.

Stamp or roll the tool on a wet finger painting.

Experiment

From a table palette of smooth paint, pick up color on the tool. Apply the color on any clean dry paper or fabric.

Pick up color from the table and apply it on a wet finger painting.

Stamp or roll clean printing tools over a multicolored painting. If you wish, clean the tool between prints.

*Elmer's Glue-All, Fuller's All Purpose Glue, Testor's White Glue, LePage's White Glue.

Grade 3, Makefield School, Yardley, Pennsylvania.

Grade 3, Makefield School.

Use paint transfer tools to add finger paint to a tool.

Print over undercoats of crayon, chalk, water color or tempera.

Apply several finger-paint colors to a tool before printing.

Combine tools for variety. Print in separate areas or overprint.

Combine hand motions with tool impressions.

Work with and without a paper cushion under the printing paper. Compare your reactions as well as the print results.

Consider ways of making some tools more durable.

Repeat a stamped print horizontally, vertically or diagonally.

Guide a roller in any direction. Feel free to over-print in the same direction or in another.

Apply the lifted print process in printing some block designs. Use a paint transfer tool to color the block and a print transfer tool to press on the back of the printing paper which covers the colored block surface of raised or recessed designs.

Work for variety in tool construction. Try soft materials on hard blocks or rollers, firm materials on soft bases. Combine materials of the same thickness on a block or roller.

Work for variety in printing methods. Push or pull the tool; observe differences when various tool motions are employed.

Be aware of the differences in working with soft and hard tools, with absorbent materials and with those that repel moisture.

Vary tool impressions by notching edges of cardboards, felt, rubber or vegetable slabs.

Collect objects with which to make recessed impressions in nonhardening clay. Work with soft and hard clay. Find ways to change or control the clay consistency.

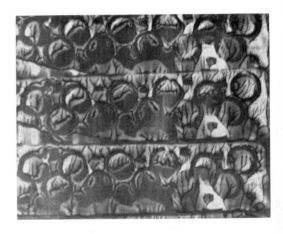

Learn to measure and mark areas for design repeats or for color registration.

Do not reject or discard tools you find unsatisfactory for finger-paint explorations. Save them for trials with other media.

Discuss conditions which affect the print results:
    consistency of finger paint
    amount of paint
    paint transfer method
    printing method
    source and amount of pressure
    characteristics of printing paper or fabric
    choice of paint color or colors
    choice of paint color values
    weather

Be an inventor, but remember that inventors do not accept theories. They contemplate, speculate and experiment continuously. They realize that results from explorations are not always satisfactory, but should be a challenge for further trials.

63

Photograph, courtesy of Reino Randall, Associate Professor of Art,
Central Washington State College, Ellensburg, Washington.

Chapter Seven
SIMPLE SCREEN PRINTING

Printing with simple tools such as stamping blocks and rollers, for initial experiences can lead to progressive experiences continually more challenging to increase interest and learning.

Throughout the grades, students' needs often require many identical copies of a design for signs, posters, greeting cards, book, program or menu covers, visual aids or decorations.

Screen printing can be adapted to any grade level. It can be an activity involving available inexpensive or discarded materials or one using materials sold expressly for the process.

Process

Serigraphy or screen printing is a method of printing by which thick paint is forced through a fabric screen stretched taut and attached to a frame. A stencil or a resist material is affixed to the screen to block out lines or shapes that paint cannot penetrate. Different materials can be used for frames, for screens and for resisting the paint. Each has uses and possibilities. Explore all to be familiar with the materials and the methods. Start with easily procured materials and simple methods.

Materials for Frames

Lumber
Wooden frames
Embroidery hoops

Cardboard boxes
Paper plates
Cardboard mats

Fabrics for Screens

Silk
Scrim

Organdy
Mesh

Marquisette
Dotted swiss

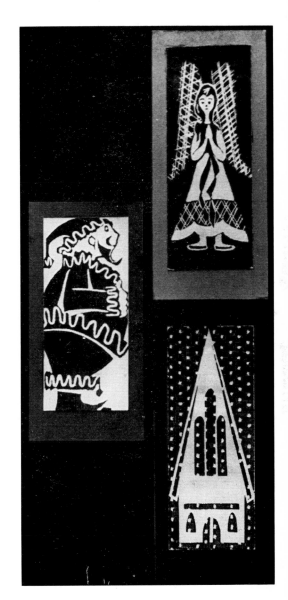

Fasteners

Stapler	Glue	Screws
Staples	Cement	Hinges
Tacks	Hammer	Screw driver

Cutting Tools

Scissors	Blades

Squeegees

Hard rubber	Finger	Beveled wood
Cardboard	Plastic	Bristle brush

Paints

Ready-mixed finger paint   Finger-paint powder

Papers

Gummed tape —for screen edges and for cardboard squeegees.

Newspaper or stencil paper —for stencils.

White, colored and novelty papers —for printing.

Resist Materials

Wax crayons	Gummed seals	String
Nail polish	Newsprint	Thick shellac

Miscellaneous

Glycerin —to retard the drying time of finger paint.

Baseboard —for two or more color registrations. Make it larger than the wooden frame to which it will be hinged.

Textures —to place under the screen for rubbings when crayon resist is used on the screen.

Pellon	—a pressed fabric which does not fray when cut.
Shellac	—for a protective coat on prints.
Tempera	—to mix with finger paint when a very wide range of colors is needed. Add gold or silver tempera to finger paint for a metallic color quality.

Experiment with Frame Making

Learn to stretch a fabric screen taut across the underside of a frame and to fasten it securely with staples or tacks. Have the warp run lengthwise, or follow the warp direction when using a squeegee to improve registration.

Use fasteners on all sides of a wooden frame.

Use staples on all edges of the opening in a flat cardboard frame.

Slit corners to flatten a cardboard box lid frame. Staple a screen across the open window in the box. Raise and tape the corners in their original position after the screen is stapled.

Add masking tape borders on the top and the bottom of the screen to provide measured, clean edges.

Cut a window in a strong paper plate. Staple a fabric screen to the window edges then add a masking tape border.

Collect embroidery hoops of wood or metal and of assorted sizes and shapes.

Use adhesive or masking tape between the hoops when one does not fit tightly in the other.

Explore different fabrics for screens.

Let masking tape or brown gummed tape block out any unwanted outer areas of a screen attached to an oval or circular hoop frame.

Experiment with Resist Materials

Wax crayons —use a finely woven screen of organdy or silk for heavy applications of crayon. If you wish, use a pre-planned design on paper as a guide under the fabric screen.

Experiment with crayon rubbings of textures placed under the screen. Rub hard or apply several crayon coats using the side of an unwrapped crayon to record the texture.

Combine crayon lines with solid areas and texture rubbings on one screen.

Feel free to use rulers or other supporting edges in making crayon designs.

Nail polish —use a finely woven screen.

Make a pencil outline on the screen.

Hold the screen away from the table while applying polish.

Paint on several coats for opaque areas; use free brush strokes or stipple for texture. Learn about consistencies of different makes of nail polish. Expose polish to air to thicken it.

Shellac —thicken shellac by letting some air-dry in a metal lid. Color it with a little paint, if you wish. Apply it as you would apply nail polish.

String —dip string in shellac or glue— or brush the adhesive on string before arranging it on the underside of a screen. Let the adhesive and string dry before printing.

Paper —cut sheets of printed or unprinted newspaper a bit larger than the screen size.

Start with simple stencils cut out of folded paper. Progress to other stencil designs cut out with sharp blades or knives.

Adhere paper stencils to screens of any fabric by placing the screen on a moist stencil and pulling finger paint across the top of the screen with a squeegee. Let the applied stencil dry for a moment or two before making more prints.

Combine paper and crayon resist methods on organdy or silk screens.

Test the adhesive qualities of gummed seals and notebook reinforcements for possible use with original paper stencils.

Experiment with Color

Paint —place two or more paint colors at one edge of the screen. Pull them across with a squeegee to merge the colors. No two free multicolored prints will be alike in color.

Use a guide system for registering a design or color area in the same position on each printing paper.

Simplify printing with two or more colors by the use of matching cross-marks on the original drawing, on each stencil and on the baseboard.

Hide flaws in registration by opaque paint or by printing a dark second color.

Explore the use of brushes, sponges, cloth pads or parts of the hand to force paint through the screen. Discover tools helpful in printing with several colors.

Accept opportunities to print unusual one-of-a-kind prints by deliberate off-registration and overlapping of color.

Vary color work by printing on original decorated papers and on colored commercial novelty papers.

Learn about commercial stencils: paper, tusche, glue block-out, Nu Film and photographic. Also investigate waterproof paints: oils, lacquers, dyes, enamels and their solvents. Visit studios and workshops to see advanced procedures.

Illustrations in this chapter, courtesy of The Studio of Binney & Smith Inc. Art Consultant, Hilda Rath.

Let experiences in simple screen printing lead to research and experimentation with commercial materials and processes for screen printing on silk, wood, glass, metal and other flat surfaces.

Grade 6, Lyndover School, Maplewood-Richmond
Heights Schools, Missouri.
Art Director, Pauline Medlen.

72

Chapter Eight
MIXED MEDIA

"Every child and adult is capable of artistically significant expression in at least one medium. Programs of art education which are adequate in scope and sufficient in intensity permit each individual to find himself through experiences in a variety of media and to develop greater ability in those he prefers."*

Essential Materials

Finger paint	Colored ink	Powder paint
Wax crayon	Colored pencils	Tempera
Pressed crayon	Water color	Chalk

Optional Materials

Oil paint	Textures	Vinyl paint
Oil	Clay	Nail polish
Lacquer	Rubber cement	Modeling mixtures
Fabrics	Household cement	Natural materials

Papers and Fabrics

Water color paper	Canvas board
Charcoal paper	Stencil paper
Colored tissue**	Novelty paper

All papers and fabrics listed for finger painting and monoprinting.***

*"Art Workshop Leaders Planning Guide," Howard Conant, Davis Publications, Inc., Worcester, Massachusetts.

**For information, please write to the Crystal Craft Tissue Co., Middletown, Ohio.

***Please refer to Chapters Three and Four.

Ann Franco Ferreira, Doylestown, Pennsylvania.

Age 15, Emerson, New Jersey Schools.
Supervisor of Art, Muriel Ray.

Tools

Iron	Brushes	String
Scissors	Scrapers	Spatula
Sponge	Blades	Straw

Adhesives

School white paste	Glue
Wallpaper paste	Cement

Robin, Grade 3, Makefield School.

Experiment with Waxed Crayon

Overlay —use crayon colors lightly to add transparent color to a dry finger painting.

Apply crayon heavily for shiny areas or for opaque lines or areas.

Use stencils and crayon to repeat a motif.

Place raised textures or shapes beneath the paper before applying crayon overlay.

Add rhythmic crayon lines on dry finger paintings or on tooled paintings or prints.

Coating —apply a light coat of crayon on absorbent paper to seal the surface and make it useful for finger painting.

74

Etching	—collect nail files, nails, single-edged blades, plastic scraps, pieces of metal or combs to use as scraping tools.

Cover a dry painting with a heavy coat of one or more crayon colors. Contrast the overcoat colors. Explore other color or value combinations. Scrape away the crayon to let sections of the finger painting appear.

Place raised textures or shapes under the paper before scraping.

Use crayon etching on sections of a painting. |

Hugh, Grade 5, Makefield School, Yardley, Pennsylvania. Art Teacher, Ann F. Thompson.

Resist	—apply finger paint mixed with water, over crayon work.
Encaustic	—add crayon shavings to dry painting. Cover with newsprint and press with a hot iron.

Apply melted crayon on a dry finger painting. |
| *Collage* | —paste cut-outs of crayoned papers to dry finger paintings.

Glue crayon shavings on a dry finger painting. |

*Brayer painting, paper stencils, chalk accents
on wet paint.
Dr. L. John G. Wenner, New Britain, Connecticut.*

Experiment with Chalk

Use white or colored chalks on wet finger paintings.

Finger paint over chalk on wet paper; scrape away sections of wet paint with tools or vigorous hand motions.

Color a printing paper with chalk to use for mono-prints or screen prints.

Experiment with Water-soluble Paints

Use any water-soluble paint or ink with brushes or tools on sections of wet finger paintings.

Use any water-soluble paint or ink with brushes or tools on sections of dry finger paintings.

Color strings to use for string printing or painting.

Pick up monoprints of mixed paint experiments.

Paint paper cut-outs with water colors or tempera. Print with them on wet or dry finger paintings.

Sprinkle powder paint on a wet painting for color or texture.

Mix powder paint with finger paint for palette knife work on absorbent papers.

Use tempera and stencils for opaque motifs on dry finger paintings.

Use sections of brush paintings as decorative papers for finger-painted screen prints or mono-prints.

76

Search for Peace, Victoria Bedford Betts.

Sea Anemone, Rosemarie Mandarino.

Add puddles of ink on very wet finger paintings. Tip the table or paper to move the ink. Blow through a straw to move the puddle. Use hand or tools to drag parts of the puddle into the background.

Drop puddles of water color or tempera paints on wet paintings. Make the puddles move.

Add color to printing tools with tempera before stamping them on wet or dry finger-painted backgrounds.

With tempera on a sponge, stamp crisp prints over line designs in wet or on dry finger paintings.

Pat damp printing tools in dry powder paint to add variety in color and texture to stamped prints on wet finger paint.

Rosemarie Mandarino.

THESE TWO FACING PAGES SHOW EXAMPLES OF
TOOLED LIFTED MONOPRINTS ACCENTED WITH
WATER COLOR AND TEMPERA PAINTS. SEE PAGE
38 FOR EXPLANATION OF THE PROCESS.

The Guardsman, Rosemarie Mandarino.

St. Nicholas, Helen Elder.

Cut paper

—pat plain or novelty paper cut-outs on a wet finger painting.

Paste or glue dimensional forms of paper or cardboard on dry paintings.

Use sections of dry finger paintings for paper mosaics, paper sculpture, stabiles, mobiles, ornaments, lettering. Select sections for miniatures.

Grade 3, Makefield School.

Press cut shapes of colored tissue on wet paintings. Smooth or wrinkle the tissue as you wish. Overlap colors. Try crayon, paint or ink lines for accents or definitions when the paint is dry.

Place cut or torn papers on a wet finger-painted background. Apply another color of paint over the layout. Remove the paper shapes while the paint is wet to let the background paint color reappear.

Janet, Grade 3, Makefield School, Yardley, Pennsylvania.

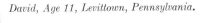
David, Age 11, Levittown, Pennsylvania.

Central High School, Trenton, New Jersey.
Art Teacher, Daphne Koenig.

Arrange pressed leaves and grasses on a dry finger-painted background. Cover with thin tissue. With a stiff brush, apply a mixture of two parts water to one part of Elmer's Glue-All over the entire tissue.

Paste a top layer of pieces of a dry finger painting on a papier-mâché craft.

Textures  —sprinkle sand, oatmeal, confetti, sparkle, etc., on wet paintings of thick paint. Pat the materials into the paint.

Pat fabric cut-outs on a wet painting.

Paste fabric cut-outs on a dry painting.

Modeling	—use finger paint to color modeling mixtures using paper, salt, flour, sand or sawdust.
	Mix finger paint with plaster of Paris and water to provide a colored mixture for dipping string.
	Instead of discarding a wet finger painting, tear it apart and soak it for a colored pulp.
	Mix finger paint with moist self-hardening clay.

Experiment for Continuous Learning

Transparency	—with brush and oil, paint areas of a finger-paint paper and let them dry. Wet the sheet of paper and apply finger paint. Hold the dry painting to the light to learn how oil affects paper.
	Cover a dry painting with a coat of oil.
Resist	—Block out designs with rubber cement on finger-paint paper. Do a finger painting. Rub off the cement when the painting is dry.
	Drip or paint household cement or lacquer on dry finger-paint paper. Finger paint over the dry cement or lacquer.

Painting

—add puddles of water to a wet finger painting. Blow through your mouth or through a straw to direct the movement of the water. Tilt the table or the paper to move the water. Combine methods.

With any brush, repeat hand motions and impressions in a wet finger painting.

With any brush, try various strokes on a smooth wet finger-painted background.

Use scraping tools to scratch away lines or areas of dry paintings. Work carefully to avoid paper damage.

Use a damp cloth or sponge to wash off sections of dry finger paintings.

Suggestions

Let mixed media explorations with finger paint lead to combinations of other media.

Visit wallpaper and fabric departments in chain and department stores to see work of commercial designers. Compare their techniques with your own and those of your classmates.

Visit art museums and galleries. Observe fine artists' ways of using media and tools.

Venture into new fields by searching for new painting or printing surfaces. Plan for future experimentation by discovering media and tools not supplied by the school. Work to develop skills with new and different kinds of materials.

Recall, Victoria Bedford Betts.

Collage, Rosemarie Mandarino.

Chapter Nine
VARIOUS VENTURES

"Finger painting can be done fast, spontaneously, almost instinctively, but there is no reason why thought and planning should not precede the quick action of the fingers."*

In all explorations with the finger-paint medium, introduce new terms with explanations and visual aids whenever possible. If classifications are not clarifications, let the students suggest other identifications that make for better understanding.**

Miniature, Henrietta Crossman.

In each activity, include the use of art principles, art elements, as well as many materials for variety in expression. Use the vocabulary of art, geared to the student's level, in discussions and demonstrations.

Miniature, Ruth Faison Shaw.

Art Principles

Design	—a pleasing arrangement within a limited area; design involves the use of:
Balance	—symmetrical or equal balance; asymmetrical or unequal balance.
Harmony	—similarity of art elements, in pleasing combinations.
Emphasis	—a center of interest in a design.

*Ralph Fabri, The City College of New York, "Today's Art," January, 1962.

**"Finger Painting," originally named by Ruth Shaw's students, has sometimes been identified as magic painting, rhythm painting, manipulative painting or hand painting.

Screen Print, Alice Sciore.

Proportion	—relationship of sizes and spaces, both in line and form.
Repetition	—of basic elements in a design.
Rhythm	—movement or continuity through repetition.
Unity	—over-all effect of each element—to the whole.
Variety	—difference in shape, size, texture.

Art Elements

Line	—indicates action, defines shape, develops symbols, provides decorative effects.
Shape	—an area confined by edges or lines.
Form	—gives a third dimension to shape.
Space	—an area between lines, shapes or forms.
Textures	—the quality of a surface; may be actual or simulated.
Tone	—the degree of lightness and darkness.
Color	—has qualities of hue (the individual colors), value (tone, tints, shades), intensity (brightness or dullness of a color).

Developing Skills

Offer a challenge for growth by leading from one experience into another. Provide for changing interests and points of view as children grow.

Paper crafts —cover and bind books; cover cartons, wastebaskets, lamp shades.

Construct kites and other paper toys.

Save cardboards cut from frozen food cartons for miniatures.

Mount or mat miniatures; make different kinds of dimensional paper frames.

Package an assortment of paintings for gift wrappings.

Paint directly on cardboard paint buckets. Use them as containers for waste paper, greeting cards, cookies. Turn them into lamp shades.

Sculpture hand-painted papers for masks, figures, favors or decorations.

Fold and fasten finger-painted papers to transform them into gay bags for gifts; paint directly on glazed white or colored commercial bags. Use them for gifts, puppets, stuffed figures.

Finger-painted covers and bindings.

Decorative brayer prints.
Photograph, courtesy of Reino Randall,
Associate Professor of Art,
Central Washington State College,
Ellensburg, Washington.

Elephants, Arnold Hall.

Landscape, Rosemarie Mandarino.

89

Finger paint on coated paper plates. When dry, cut some apart for mobile or stabile sections or for sculptures.

Employ measuring, planning and painting skills in mural making.

Finger paint on washable wallpaper for murals, screen panels, puppet theatre stage sets, diorama and display backgrounds.

Cover all or part of a painting with colored cellophane to change color impressions.

Weave cut or folded strips of finger-painted papers for mats. Weave strips in and out of wire screening with an open mesh. Utilize open mesh screening for display panels, lamp shades and other constructions.

Helpful hints

—add glycerin to finger paint to retard the drying when working on a large surface or for detailed work.

Review papers listed in previous chapters. Select a paper suitable for the painting process and the craft function.

90

Fabric crafts — finger paint glazed fabrics to use as hangings, place mats, book covers. Test samples of fabric before planning the craft.

Cut and sew costumes of finger-painted fabrics for dolls, puppets and people.

Sew or drape backgrounds and stage curtains for puppet theatres.

Design and assemble stuffed toys.

Use burlap, buckram and other firm fabrics for lifted monoprints. Add stitchery, appliqué, or other materials when definition or emphasis is needed or desired.

Print or paint with tools and finger paint on any firm fabric. Starch limp fabrics before use.

Measure wastebaskets, lamp shades, screens and home accessories. Make paper patterns to use as guides for fabric work.

Helpful hints — thin finger paint with water for use on fabrics. Thick paint will crack and chip when folded or handled.

Apply clear shellac on articles that may come in contact with moisture.

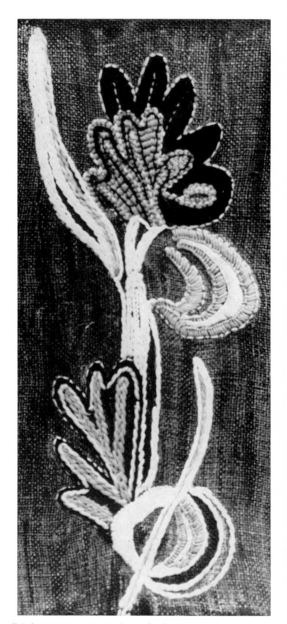

Stitchery over a monoprint on burlap,
Catherine Moore Pilley,
Llanerch, Havertown, Pennsylvania.

Mexican Wood Crafts, painting with tools.

Wood crafts —construct toys, furniture,* wastebaskets, racks, trays, book ends.

Collect strips and moldings for picture, tray or screen frames. Use strips or dowels for hangings; use assorted forms for toys.

Buy smooth unpainted bread boards to use for plaques, tie, belt and key racks.

Saw and sand lumber scraps for wood crafts.

Helpful hints —give unpainted wood a thin coat of shellac before finger painting on the wood surface.

Work directly on flat oil or rubber-based paint.

Shellac tempera-painted wood before using finger paint.

Sand glazed surfaces.

Smooth finger paint and mix colors on a table palette before applying finger paint on wood.

*Please investigate "grained furniture" to learn how our early settlers decorated furniture with combs, feathers or wads of paper.

Plastic crafts —clean and test many kinds of plastics to learn which hold and which resist finger paint. Test bleach containers, sheets of dull finish and frosted plastic, firm Fiberglass, molded Polyethylene food, water and waste containers, fabric and adhesive-backed plastics, commercial lamp shades.

Sand plastics to clean them and to remove a high glaze.

Turn plastic bottles into figures. Dress some with painted papers or fabrics.

Make ornaments by cutting shapes out of containers.

Save scrap cut-outs for mobile-making.

Use sheet plastics for mats, transparencies, lamp shades, sculptures.

Consider adhesive-backed plastics for mural-making. Use the chalkboard for a working surface and white or colored "Con-tact"* for a painting surface. Sand the surface before applying finger paint.

*"Con-tact" is sold in food, chain and department stores. For further information, please write to: Cohn-Hall-Marx Co., 40 West 40th Street, New York 18, New York.

*Photograph, courtesy of Anna Dunser,
Richmond Heights, Missouri.*

Helpful hints	—paint directly on large areas; rub paint smooth on a table, for small areas.

Spray or brush on clear shellac when the article needs a protective coat.

For permanent transparencies, cover the dry paint with self-laminating plastic sheets that have either shiny or non-glare surfaces.*

Experiment for Continuous Learning

Blueprint —finger paint on glass. Place blueprint paper or sepia positive paper under the glass or against dry finger paint on a window. Try different time exposures. Wash paper in a pan of water.

Photogram —finger paint on a piece of glass. In a dark room, place the glass on contact or enlarging paper. Expose briefly to light. Bathe the paper, face down, in developer; wash through a stop bath for 5 to 10 seconds; immerse in an acid fixer for the same time. Thoroughly wash away all traces of chemicals under running water. Dry prints on an absorbent surface.**

*For information, please write to Carr Plastics Corporation, 3407 Prospect Avenue, Cleveland 15, Ohio.

**Please consult local camera shops for chemical and paper supplies.

94

| Glass | —finger paint on containers, windows, scraps of clean glass. Spray or brush shellac when a protective coat is needed. Apply self-laminating plastic sheets when permanence is required. |
| | |

Glass

—finger paint on containers, windows, scraps of clean glass. Spray or brush shellac when a protective coat is needed. Apply self-laminating plastic sheets when permanence is required.

Finger-painted glass is useful for screen panels, room dividers, aquarium walls. Paint on the air side of glass aquariums.

Parchment

—use as a finger-painting paper. Measure, cut and assemble lamp shades.

Cork

—apply a thin coat of shellac to provide a better working surface. Adhere the painted cork to an article with rubber cement or glue.

Metal

—work as on a glass surface. Shape metal into containers or tack metal on a base before applying finger paint.*

Ceramic plate from Italy.

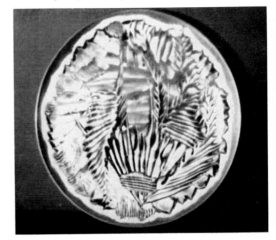

Ceramics

—make a glaze by mixing one part dry finger paint powder, two parts borax and four parts water. Use a heavy application immediately on bisque or green ware. Fire at approximately cone 07. Test firing ranges as well as colors to observe the changes. Learn the limitations of non-toxic colors.

*Any water-based paint is more decorative than functional when applied on a non-absorbent material.

Helpful Tools for Large Ventures

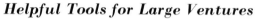

Stiff arm   —sturdy cardboard tubes covered with chamois, rubber, felt, sponge cloth. Hold with the hand or use fat ones as arm gloves.

Brayers   —single and double brayers, rollers for interior wall paints, rollers covered with textured materials or with raised lines or shapes.

Gloves   —fabric, rubber, thin plastic.*

*For information, please write to Hammacher-Schlemmer, 145 East 57th Street, New York, New York.

Blocks	—of wood; carve designs in the wood or add raised designs of textured materials, rubber or felt. Glue materials on sponge blocks or on cardboard boxes.
Stencils	—for repetition. Apply paint with a dry brush technique, with sponge or fabric pads, or with brayers.
Squeegees	—of rubber, beveled wood, firm, backed felt, linoleum, firm and flexible plastics. Cut away sections of an edge to produce stripes in the paint.
Beater	—hand or electric mixer—to mix large quantities of new colors, to mix adhesives with finger paint, to mix a thinner paint by adding water.

Victoria Bedford Belts.

"Seven Things for a Craftsman to Remember

"The Value of Time;

The Success of Perseverance;

The Pleasure of Working;

The Dignity of Simplicity;

The Virtue of Patience;

The Improvement of Talent;

The Joy of Originating."*

Through craft activity, the student learns to respect workers because he has experienced thinking, feeling, planning, experimenting, creating, testing. Through craft activity he has opportunities to select a hobby that gives satisfaction, absorbs leisure time, is enjoyed by others, has practical applications and offers new means of expression.

*Marshall Field.

Circuit of Space, Oil, by Irene Rice Pereira.
Photograph, courtesy of Syracuse University Collection, New York.
Laurence Schmeckebier, Professor of Fine Arts and Director of the School of Art.

Meadow Round, Oil, by Irving Kaufman.
Photograph, courtesy of Rehn Gallery, New York City.
Professor Kaufman, Art Director, College of Architecture and Design, The University of Michigan, Ann Arbor.

98

Chapter Ten
THE ARTIST EXPLORES

"To identify with materials so that one learns to predict the behavior of media in order to use them creatively is like an intimate friendship. It is needless to say such close relationship must result in love and deep affection for the medium of expression."*

Appreciation and Growth

Study the many movements of art expression throughout the ages. Study the works of artists in all media.

Investigate the development of an artist. Learn to recognize art elements and feel them. Look for design elements, focus of interest, contrast, relationship of line and shape, subordination of related parts.

Strive to develop refined perception or sensibilities. Grow in the capacity to receive varied impressions: visual, structural, tactile, kinesthetic, auditive, esthetic, social, emotional, and intellectual.

Realize that understanding means knowledge from the combined use of the senses.

Think about the motivations and the intentions of artists.

Detect paintings which express ideas rather than the mastery of a special technique.

Observe the continuous experimentation of artists and the use of different techniques to express changing attitudes.

*Viktor Lowenfeld, *School Arts Magazine*, October, 1959.

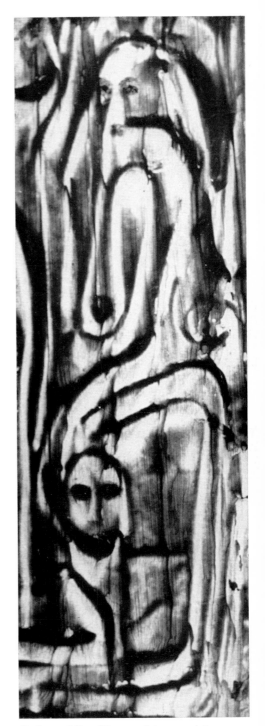

Father and Son, Finger paint monoprint, Victoria Bedford Betts.

Spanish Landscape, a color woodblock,
Paul Rene Gauguin.

Be aware of freedom in the choice and in the use of materials, tools, media or techniques in contemporary art work.

Examine the choice and use of materials to learn if they serve the artist's purpose.

Since sensitivities differ in expression and in meaning with each artist and with each work of the artist, weigh the thought that each creative work has its own esthetic standard.

Color

Constantly observe color in nature.

Learn all you can about color sources, properties, reactions and influences.

Discover examples which show that color choice is determined by feeling rather than reality. Look for personal rather than popular uses of color.

String around a woodblock, used as a stamp over a sponged background.
Tempera painting by Burt Wasserman, Glassboro State College, New Jersey.

100

Applications

It is stimulating to review some of the recognitions of finger paint in the fields of fine and commercial art:

One-man shows in fine art galleries.

Group shows in galleries and in universities.

Full page illustrations for the advertising field.

Story illustrations in leading magazines. These often were abstractions, to create an impression or establish a mood.

Titles-in-action to introduce films and television programs.

Reproductions of designs for wallpapers, textiles and plastics.

Reproductions of designs for note papers, greeting cards, book jackets and menus.

Original paintings and panels used as backgrounds for photographing clothing fashions or furniture and for window display.

Original paintings and murals on walls of homes, offices and salons.

Consider the review as a pause for refreshment and revitalization before taking another step. Let all explorations and achievements be stepping stones to new adventures.

Photograph, courtesy of
Ravel Perfume Corporation, New York City.

Ruth Faison Shaw, the originator of the medium, had the first showing of finger paintings. It was presented by the Ferargil Galleries in 1940. In her book, "Finger Painting and How I Do It," Miss Shaw says: "Finger Painting is not, nor does it purport to be a short cut to other types of painting, art without tears, as it were. Creative work must come from imagination and personal experience. But to understand the nature of a medium and its logical use is important, if one is to derive the greatest benefit from it."

Miniature.

Ruth Faison Shaw, Chapel Hill, North Carolina.

Sara Ravndal Smith was closely associated with Ruth Shaw both in Europe and America. Appropriately, her paintings were shown in the 1940 exhibition of finger paintings at the Ferargil Galleries.

103

Mystery.

Aqua Marine.

Victoria Bedford Betts, associated with Ruth Shaw since 1934, has worked with the medium since then. She has had solo shows at The Art Club of St. Petersburg, Florida, and The Museum of New Mexico in Santa Fe, and has participated in many group shows.

Mrs. Betts first pictured her Florida childhood in finger paint and worked from memory rather than from model. In the past decade she has expressed the rovings of her imagination in monoprint ventures.

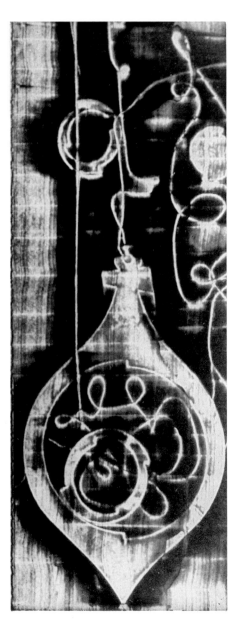

The Little Minstrel.

105

Rosemarie Mandarino, a talented artist in all media, was associated with Victoria Betts for fifteen years. Her paintings have been shown in many college and university galleries and include sensitive expressions with varied techniques.

Rosemarie Mandarino, New York City.

Wings, Faith Vilas.
Photographs, courtesy of Charles Vilas,
Branford, Connecticut.

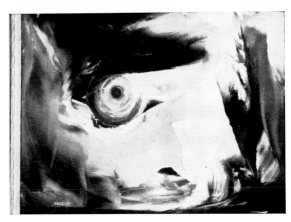

Genese, Faith Vilas.

Faith Vilas believed "that in an age awakening to Atomic Force and Nuclear Energy, the creative artist must not be content to paint old subject matter even if he tries to give it a new flavor by twist and distortion. He must capture for his canvas the future, the unknown; he must project his vision into the unexplored dimensions just beginning to lift above the horizons."

Mrs. Vilas has had 38 solo exhibits since 1944. Her work has been shown at The Pen and Brush Club of New York, The Ferargil Gallery, New York City, The Washington, D.C., Arts Club and in galleries abroad. Sheldon Cheney wrote: "I had the pleasure of a considerable visit with Mrs. Vilas. It was a real experience and a day to remember. There is unforgettable beauty in her pictures and I shall not attempt analysis of what it is that makes them beautiful or memorable or haunting."

Kathleen Caffee Dickinson of Winter Haven, Florida, has worked with the medium for thirty years. She often worked with a pre-conceived plan and with a landscape or model in actual sight. After passing through periods of palm trees and moonlight, bird study, lush vegetation and figures, Mrs. Dickinson wrote in 1962: "What I'd like best to do would be paintings for use in religious context. I think particularly of chapels in hospitals and am working toward this. Already I have some of my paintings in chapels and churches. One is painted directly on a plastered wall with finger paints mixed with wood filler and tempera and used with large brushes."

Blue Madonna, Kathleen Caffee Dickinson.

Irene Laverty, Philadelphia, Pennsylvania.

White Herons, Kathleen Caffee Dickinson.

110

Irene Laverty, designer of fabrics, has exhibited at The Philadelphia Art Alliance, The Museum of Art and The Museum College of Art in Philadelphia where she was presented the Alumni Design Award for her outstanding contribution as a designer of fabrics. She uses all mediums in her work and "believes that finger paint, with its capacity for freedom and control, is a workable, important contribution to new creative design."

111

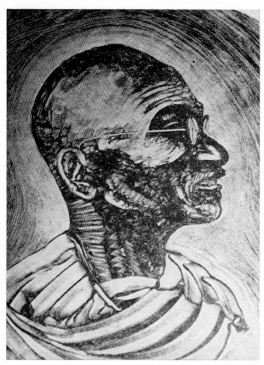

Gandhi, Andres Bueso.

Andres Bueso of San Juan, Puerto Rico, has achieved fame in Puerto Rico as a painter and as a sculptor. He writes: "Finger painting is an adventure full of discoveries. An exciting medium of expression, it challenges the imagination and stimulates the creative ability of the artist."

Mr. Bueso presented his adventures in a solo show at the Arthur U. Newton Galleries in New York City in 1948. His subjects include flowers, sea life, landscapes, animals and portraits.

Gertrude Lawrence (Mrs. Richard Aldrich), inspired actress, studied with Ruth Shaw. Her paintings often captured and portrayed mood. Miss Lawrence exhibited in a number of group shows.

Sonata, Gertrude Lawrence.

112

Francis R. Fast wrote about finger painting: "The trained artist has much to gain from an understanding of its use, and it can be a fortifying and valuable adjunct to his own work. It is an appraisal, as it were, of one's senses of rhythm, form and color." "It is difficult to predict what the future for finger painting may be, though constant experiment merely tends to widen the far horizon of its possibilities."

Mr. Fast began to paint in 1942. He has had fifteen one-man exhibitions, among them solos at The Charles Morgan Gallery, New York City, the Robert C. Vose Galleries in Boston, The Montclair, New Jersey, Art Museum and The Currier Gallery of Art in Manchester, New Hampshire.

Stuart M. Shaw, New York City.

Miniature, Clyde C. Clack, Dallas, Texas.
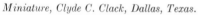

114

Sascha Brastoff, Los Angeles, California.

Charles Colahan.

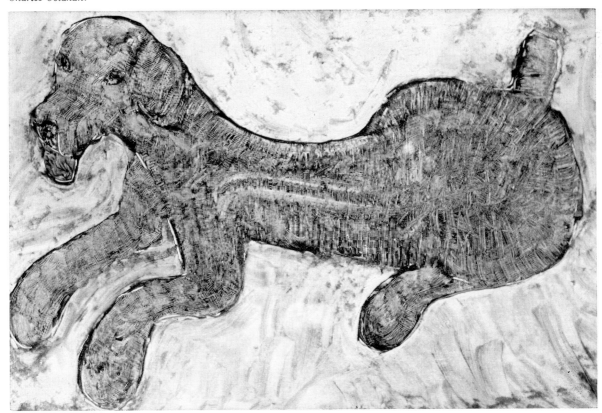

Miniatures, Anna Dunser,
Richmond Heights, Missouri.

Monotype, Jane Rehnstrand, Superior, Wisconsin.

116

Gilda K. Hoffmann.

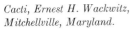
*Cacti, Ernest H. Wackwitz,
Mitchellville, Maryland.*

*Miniature, Harry Greenwell, Kalamazoo, Michigan.
Photograph, courtesy of Mrs. Alfred W. Lyons.*

*Misty Glen, Mary Beth Wackwitz (Mrs. E. H.),
Supervisor of Art, Prince George's County,
Upper Marlboro, Maryland.*

117

Natalie Bixby.

Luigi Lucioni.

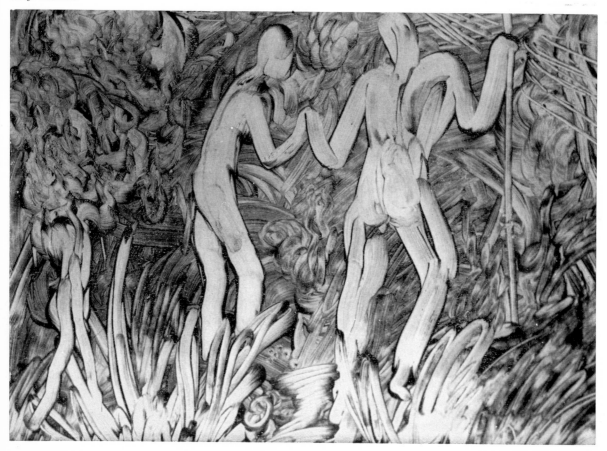

Allen T. Terrell.

Allie Kitchens MacDanald, Miami, Florida.

119

Clowns, Henry Ray.

Dr. Henry W. Ray, Assistant Superintendent, Bucks County Schools, Pennsylvania, has done much in experimental and creative photography. The finger-paint medium also has challenged his inventive mind. He feels that "finger painting is the poetry of the visual arts. The medium literally 'explodes' into forms. Color harmonies evolve with magical ease and the painting is completed while the emotional motivation is still afire."

*Central Park, Arnold Hall.**

*Please refer to page 89 for another example of Mr. Hall's work.

120

Distinguished pioneers, whose work is included in this chapter, painted their examples about thirty years ago. They are: Stuart M. Shaw, Arnold Hall, Charles Colahan, Allan Terrell, Natalie Bixby and Luigi Lucioni.

Artists whose paintings were executed about twenty years ago are: Sascha Brastoff, Allie K. MacDanald and Geneva MacDonald.

Countless other artists and teachers have explored the medium for their own expression and to increase their understanding of and ability to direct the creative work of their students.

White Bird, Geneva MacDonald, Boston, Massachusetts.

The Royal Family, Henry Ahrens, Yardley, Pennsylvania.

121

Chapter Eleven
EVALUATION AND EXHIBITION

*"If a man does not keep pace with his companions, perhaps it is because he hears a different drummer. Let him step to the music which he hears, however measured or far away."** *

Evaluation

Work habits, attitude, progress or satisfactory growth in art experiences should be noted by the classroom teacher as well as by the art specialist. They should know the student as well as his work. Evaluation should take place whenever it is needed during a learning situation: by the student or teacher during the activity, by a joint discussion of the completed work, and by a study of the exhibited work.

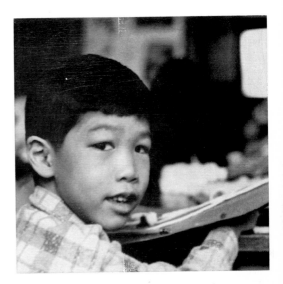

In an appraisal, consider growth in:

Enjoyment	Knowledge of processes
Awareness	Confidence
Inventiveness	Judgment
Manipulative skills	Appreciation

*"To evaluate is to distinguish between the important and the unimportant. Importance is gauged by objectives. What is important for one purpose may be unimportant for another. Value or importance may depend upon a wide variety of factors. In dealing with things, value is determined by physical factors, in some instances small, in others large. In dealing with human problems, value will depend upon personality factors, sometimes obvious, sometimes obscure."***

*Henry David Thoreau.
**Dr. G. Lake Imes, *Think Magazine*, February, 1951.

Creative Art in Education Clinic,
School of Art, Syracuse University, New York.
Photographs, courtesy of Dr. Michael F. Andrews.

Exhibition

Appreciation of creative work by other students and by artists, through display, can be a motivating factor in the organization of students' work for classroom, school building, home and community exhibits.

Boxes, folders, folios can be made by the students to be used as individual or classroom storage units. These are valuable aids for the classroom teacher and for the art specialist in reviewing activities and also in assembling work for exhibition.

An exhibition should be a learning device, planned to fill the needs of the observers. It should catch attention and hold it by being interesting and helpful. The ideal display is simple to set up, strong for its purpose and truthful.

In any type of display, from the student telling about his work during and after the process, to mounted formal exhibitions, remember that vision is influenced by the personality of the observer.

Plan Ahead

Look for temporary and permanent exhibit space.

Store selected display materials; file ideas.

Search for new ideas and materials.

Select a committee of helpers.

Schedule changing committees.

Provide for the preparation of explanation sheets for parents to be available at the exhibition scene.

Plan for home, newspaper and community publicity.

Invite students to be hosts—to tell about individual and group activities.

Invite the parents to cooperate—with donations or loans of display properties.

Devise ways of dividing space.

Record effective color schemes.

Show respect for the work and the worker.

Include in a display

Children's names on art work.

Readable words of explanation.

Legible signs appropriate to the display.

Signs that use action verbs: "OUR HANDS DANCE"; "WE MIX MANY COLORS".

Sensitive use of color combinations. Be aware that color impressions are changed by their surroundings: by neighboring colors, lines, shapes or forms.

Colors to stimulate emotions and interpret ideas. Use quiet harmonies for some needs, shocking ones for others. Consider the use of related colors (which contain a common hue), opposing colors (which contain no common hue), cool or recessive colors, warm or advancing colors.

Any kind of materials assembled according to a plan, provided they contribute to learning: sensory experiences, different painting surfaces, varied background surfaces, two-dimensional work, eye-catching motifs that relate to the display.

Relationships; group paintings to emphasize the meaning of the art work. Arrange paintings so that the eye moves from one to another.

Create a large unit of design on each display area.

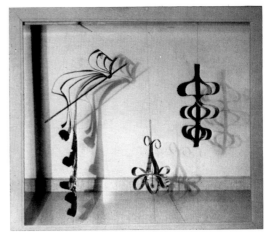

125

DESIGN
DESIGN

LINE

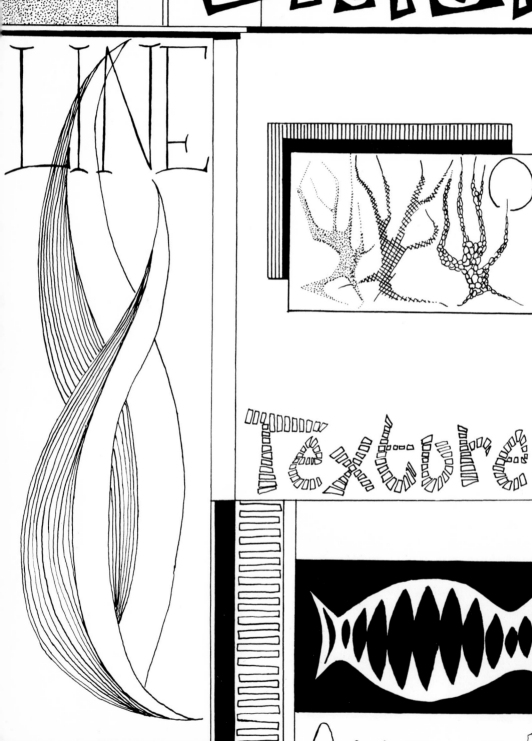

Shape

texture

CONTRAST

MATS

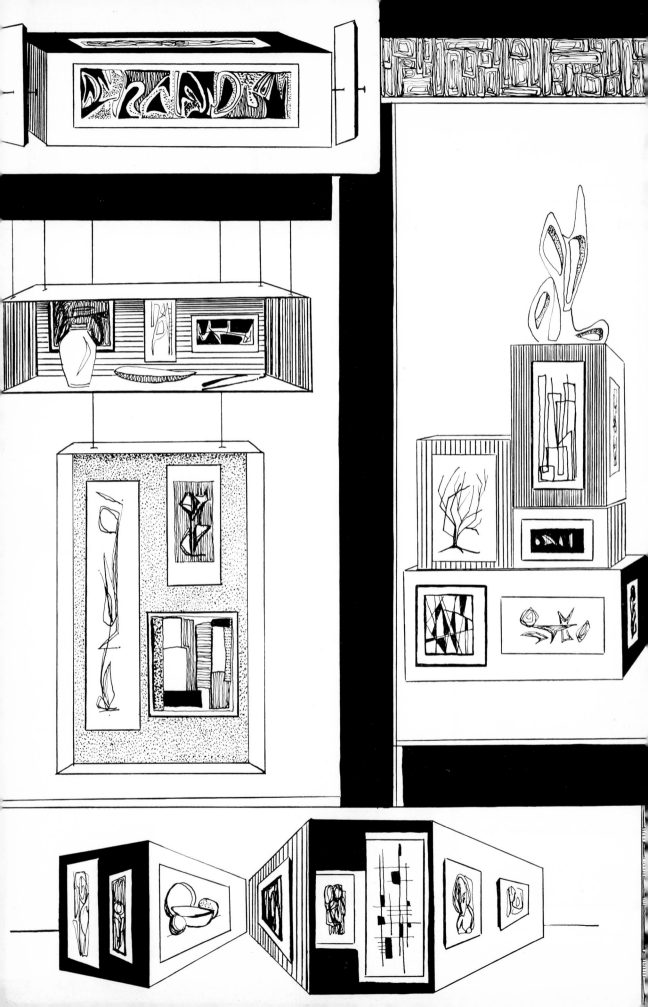

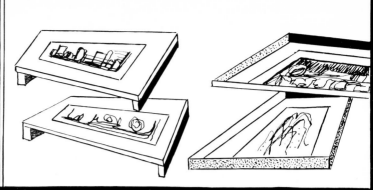

PROPS

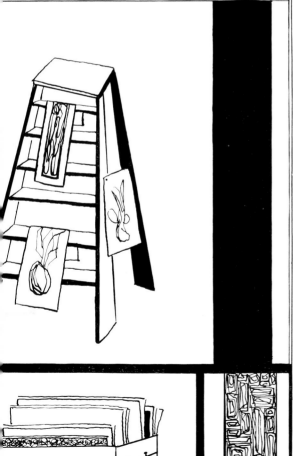

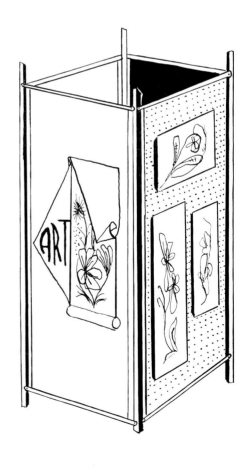

ART

FOLIOS

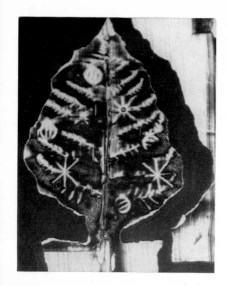

Suggestions

Remember that students will not know whether or not art materials fit their needs until they have opportunities to explore their uses.

Request student participation in all activities: during the motivation, the activity, the evaluation and the exhibition.

Encourage thinking by well planned questions.

Guide students to involve their hearts, their heads and their hands in observation and in expression.

Appreciate their efforts.

Grade 6, The Denali School, Anchorage, Alaska.
Teacher, Grace Alexanders.
Photograph, courtesy of Alex Duff Combs, Jr.,
Supervisor of Art.

Exhibit of kindergarten finger paintings, Normandy Schools, St. Louis County, Missouri. Photograph, courtesy of Virginia R. Lacy, Supervisor of Art.

Help parents to understand and enjoy children's art experiences. Let them know that their cooperation plays a necessary and important part in the development of children's habits, attitudes, imagination, invention and performance.

Realize that many people influence child growth through art: the art teacher, the classroom teacher, school administrators, community members, family, classmates and playmates.

"The desire to explore, discover, and invent can be related to any life situation. It may even become one of the major drives, or characteristics, of a personality. Art education merely serves as a means to unfold and develop this drive, considered so vital for the free expression of man."

*"The Meaning of Creativity for Art Education," Viktor Lowenfeld, E.A.A. Research Bulletin, March, 1954.

Exhibit of sixth grade finger paintings, Normandy Schools.

Photograph, courtesy of Delbert W. Smedley, Granite School District, Salt Lake City, Utah.